For June,
come and see
us in ashland again

warmly
Frances Sharkey
24 July 1992
Ashland, Oregon

A Parting Gift

A Parting Gift

Frances Sharkey, M.D.

ST. MARTIN'S PRESS·NEW YORK

Design by Manuela Paul
10 9 8 7 6 5 4 3 2 1
First Edition

to the memory of Brian

acknowledgements

In order to ensure privacy, many of the names and locations in the book have been changed and some of the actual events disguised. But most of the conversations and the words of my dying patients were recorded indelibly in my mind when they were said, and they are accurate in spite of the passage of years.

No child comes into this world without help, and the most fortunate are those who have encouragement and love as they grow. In that, there are great similarities between a child and a book.

I would like to express my gratitude to those who helped this book take shape. Louise Samuelson's unfailing belief in me and devotion to the manuscript enabled me not only to begin, but to complete this book. Ruth Cohen and Sara Bershtel showed me that the spirit of Maxwell Perkins lives on in today's editors. Thomas McCormack masterfully separated the wheat from the chaff. Cheryl Rae Glickfield was especially helpful throughout the publishing process. Edward Goldstein, Laura Garrison, Barbara Hoover, Bob Sharkey, Ron Montana and Vince Andrew gave valuable criticism and generous encouragement. Many others read chapters and said the right thing at the right time. Doug and Karyn Samuelson and my children, Phillip, Thompson, Hicks, Carlo, Thai-Binh and Liz, kept the house running smoothly while I was with my typewriter, and richly deserve my thanks and love.

Frances Sharkey
Los Gatos, California
April 25, 1981

contents

preface

This winter when the rains come and the hills turn green David will have been dead for five years. His mother and I saw each other frequently in the months following his death. Sometimes she would stop by my office for a few minutes if she happened to be in the neighborhood. Occasionally I'd call her and drive to her house at noontime.

We'd have lunch in the dining room. A new china cabinet stood in the place where David's bed had been.

Our conversations were often a bit disjointed, as if Betty and I were aware of each other's thoughts.

"I never would have gone out if I'd known he was going to die just then," she said. "I wanted to be with him."

"I know you did," I said. "So did I."

"But sometimes I think he wanted it that way. He waited until I was gone. He knew it would be easier for me that way." Betty was silent for a few minutes, then she added, "David always loved to do things for me. That must have been his parting gift."

         o   o   o

I became a doctor because I love life. Twenty years ago, at the end of four years of medical school, I had to decide which branch of medicine to specialize in, and I felt the same love of life should be the prevailing motive in my choice. I considered everything from psychiatry to obstetrics, but I settled on pediatrics.

At the time I thought I knew my reasons clearly. When a child was ill, nature was the doctor's greatest ally in the healing process. The diseases a pediatrician was called upon to treat were mainly infectious in origin, and antibiotics were available to cure them. I enjoyed children and knew the opportunity to see them grow year by year would bring me pleasure. I made my decision without reservation.

For the next twenty years whenever I was asked why I became a pediatrician, those were the reasons I gave. It's only recently that I have realized an equally important reason for my choice of pediatrics was deeply hidden inside me.

I became a pediatrician not just because I love life. I became a pediatrician because I was afraid of death.

The recognition of how great that fear was, after years of a successful pediatric practice, surprised me.

This revelation didn't occur easily but as a result of the death of a dear eight-year-old patient of mine, David. For the first time in my career I helped a child die in his own home because that was where he chose to die. His death had a profound effect upon me and made me reexamine my previous experiences with dying children.

I found there was no question but that I had influenced the manner in which they died. As I thought about this, I realized that during the early years of my career my unrecognized fear of death had unconsciously determined many of my decisions about where and how children died.

For the first time I became aware of one of the main reasons children usually die in hospitals instead of in their own homes—and it was a disturbing insight. It is so much easier for the doctor if a child dies in a hospital. All the doctor has to do is step into the hospital room once or twice a day and check the child. Most of his time is usually spent reading the nurse's notes on the chart, writing a daily progress note and checking laboratory work, rather than talking to the child. After all, what more can be done?

In addition, the routine of a hospital is quite comforting to the doctors. There is about the impersonal hospital room a protective anonymity. It shields the doctor from the emotional impact of seeing a dying child in his very own bedroom where his life and individuality are so much in evidence.

Seemingly the parents play a part in the decision as much as the doctor does. The child never gets to make this decision for himself; the adults do it. But the parents' role in deciding is, in fact, usually nonexistent. They are almost always so devastated by what is going on that they can barely accept what is happening. They see that the doctor assumes that the child will stay in the hospital till death. It is traditional; it is "the best thing." The doctor is accepted as the expert about death. Few doctors urge the parents to take the child home, and sometimes their reason is consideration for the mother and father. It seems cruel and callous to suggest that the parents undertake the care of the child at home. The parents are rare who can bring themselves to say, "My child hates the hospital. I want him to die at home."

But I feel there are many, many instances when they should say this, and that is one of the reasons I have written this book.

I am writing it to doctors as much as to parents. I now realize that a misplaced consideration influenced me for years: I always identified more strongly with the parents who were losing their child than with the child who was losing his life. My major concern once I was certain the child was indeed going to die was to protect and spare the parents who would have to go on living.

Over twenty years ago Elisabeth Kubler-Ross published her remarkable book on the needs of dying patients. Her humanitarian genius in recognizing their problems and making them issues subject to discussion paved the way for adults to be given the choice of where they wished to die. Children are still not given that choice, and their guardians—parents and doctors—seldom consider that the child would have a preference about the intensely personal question of where he should spend his last days. Indeed, it is often automatically accepted—as it no longer is with adults—that the fact of his approaching death should not be discussed with the child.

I now believe that this whole attitude—whether it is based on blindness, selfishness or mistaken kindness—has an inhumane result that none of us really wants.

The death of a child is always, I think, the most somber event anyone ever encounters. But it is a tragedy that can be compounded by a second tragedy: the denial of death. I hope that my book will help persuade people not that there is ever a good way for a child to die, but that there are some ways that are better than others.

One

The Old Woman

Before I became a medical student I'd had no experience with death. No one close to me had died. I'd never even been to a funeral. My ideas had been formed the way most people's are—from the books I'd read, the movies I'd seen, and from my own vivid imagination.

In my first year of medical school in New York City in the late 1950s the entire year was spent in classes that dealt with basic science. It was not until my second year that I encountered death. It came during a course in physical diagnosis when I was to examine my first real patient.

I was one of a small group of students that went to a large city hospital to be assigned a patient. I would be expected to take a history of that patient's health and to do a complete physical examination and diagnose what I thought was wrong.

Despite my new white coat and stethoscope, I was very

1

nervous. I knew I looked more like a college freshman than a medical student, and I feared the patient might realize just how inexperienced I was.

The instructor in charge misinterpreted my anxiety. "Don't worry," he said. "I know this is your first patient. I'll give you a woman."

I waited while each of my classmates was given a patient's name and a chart. Finally, when the others in the group were gone, the instructor said, "I haven't forgotten you. There's a new patient who's just been admitted. The intern examined her in the emergency room, but he hasn't had time to fill out her chart yet. I want you to examine her thoroughly and write down your findings. Remember, taking a good history is ninety percent of making a correct diagnosis." He smiled and handed me a blank chart with a room number on it.

The new admission was in a private room. I stood outside the door and tried to compose myself to look as if I had been examining people for years. Then I knocked and walked in.

The room was small and bleak. A narrow hospital bed took up most of the space. On it lay an old, old woman still wearing a dress and coat. There were wrinkled cotton stockings on her spindly legs and worn house slippers on her feet. She lay on top of the sheet, a hospital gown folded neatly on the edge of the bed. Beside her, huddled together, stood two other old women who looked shaken and confused. There were no chairs in the room for them to sit on. The only other piece of furniture was an iron nightstand with chipped white paint. The overhead light was harsh, and I saw at once that there was something very wrong with the woman on the bed. Her face was gray, her breathing labored.

I hesitated to disturb her, fearing I might make her feel worse. As I stood awkwardly holding the stethoscope in my hands, the old woman opened her eyes and looked up at me. She moved her lips in a wan, almost apologetic smile, her nostrils flaring with each breath. Clearly she would never be able to answer the long list of questions I was supposed to ask. It would be better to try to get her history from the women who had brought her in.

The two women, who must themselves have been in their seventies, were standing so close together that their shoulders touched. Their faces were drawn with concern.

"Please," I asked, gesturing to the patient, "can you tell me what's wrong with her?"

One of them said in a soft voice, "She's our aunt. She lives with us. She's ninety-two and she's been sick for a long time. Her doctor came to see her at home today and said that her heart was failing." The niece moved closer to me and whispered, "He said she was dying and we'd better take her to a hospital. So we brought her here. We didn't know what else to do."

Oh my God, was all I could think. I was here to examine a patient who was supposed to be well enough to answer questions. I didn't know what to do with a patient who was dying. She needed a *real* doctor.

"Excuse me," I said. "I'll try to find the intern." I left the room and saw a nurse walking down the corridor. "My patient needs help," I told her. "Where can I find the intern?"

"He and the resident are both in the emergency room. It's busy down there, and they have several patients they're admitting. Is there anything I can do?"

"Could you ask him to come up here right away?" I said. I stood there feeling helpless and inadequate. I'd better do something. I'd been told the old woman had heart trouble. At least I could go and examine her and listen to her heart. But what would I do after that?

I hurried back into the room and began in the most obvious way. "Please help me get her undressed," I asked the nieces.

It required all three of us to take off her coat and pull her dress over her head. As I slipped the hospital gown over her thin body, I saw the pulsating beat of her heart under the dry flesh of her withered breast. Suddenly I felt terribly sad. I tucked the sheet under her arms and picked up the chart and my pen.

I had been given a long list of questions to ask. It included childhood diseases, present and past occupations, previous hospitalizations and, if the patient was a female, her menstrual cycles. That last question was certainly irrelevant, I thought. But weren't all the questions irrelevant now? The woman was ninety-two, and her doctor had said she was dying.

I shifted from foot to foot. Across the bed the two nieces looked every bit as uncomfortable as I felt. I decided not to bother with the questions on the list.

"Tell me about her," I said simply. "I meant tell me about her illness," but her nieces didn't realize that.

"Our aunt was one of the most beautiful women in the country when she was young," one of them began eagerly. "She was a model—an artist's model. Famous artists painted her. A portrait of her still hangs in the Metropolitan Museum."

"She had such lovely auburn hair," the other one added. "And we love her dearly."

The old woman on the bed did not move. Perhaps she was dozing, perhaps not. I should listen to her heart, I thought. As I put my stethoscope on her chest, I realized that I'd never heard a heart in failure. I couldn't make sense of the sounds transmitted through the stethoscope. The heartbeat was almost completely obscured by a noise like rushing water. Could this be what the books called murmurs?

While I puzzled about what I was hearing and how to describe my findings, I glanced at her face. There was a change. Her lips were now tinged with blue. She was obviously much worse than when I had first come into the room. I'd better get help right away. I closed up her gown and pulled the sheet around her. Standing up and putting the stethoscope into the pocket of my white coat, I said quietly to the nieces, "I'm going out to get the intern. I'll be right back. Don't worry."

I ran to the emergency room and found the intern talking to another doctor. Urgently I told him, "I'm a medical student on your ward and the patient assigned to me is an old woman in heart failure. I think she may be dying. I don't know what to do. Could you please come and look at her?"

He nodded. "The ninety-two year old? I'll be there as soon as I can. First I've got to admit a forty-year-old man who's had a heart attack. Go back upstairs and ask the nurse to bring the portable EKG machine into the room. Then give your patient some oxygen and examine her carefully. Don't look so worried. There's not too much we can do for someone her age."

Reluctantly I returned to the ward without him and asked the nurse to bring in an oxygen tank and an EKG machine. I had tried to make the old woman more comfortable by sitting her up and propping pillows behind her. I put an oxygen mask on her and opened the valve on the large green oxygen tank.

The nieces stood by the bed, watching me with approval. They seemed relieved to have someone else caring for her. The loudspeaker announced that afternoon visiting hours now were over, and as if that were a signal, they each kissed their aunt carefully on her wrinkled cheek, dabbed their tears and left. I thought they must know it was for the last time, but I wasn't sure.

While I watched the patient and waited for the intern, I opened my textbook to the chapter on heart failure. "It is easier for a patient to breathe in an upright position," the book said. I cranked up the head of the bed and put another pillow behind her back. The old woman smiled weakly at me, as if to thank me. "Rotating tourniquets should be used to decrease the flow of blood to the heart." There was a tourniquet on the nightstand, but I wondered with increasing desperation, how do you put on rotating tourniquets? Maybe the next part of the chapter would tell me. But it didn't. "A diuretic should be given to clear the lungs of fluid." Yes, but the intern would have to do that. What was keeping him? "The patient should be digitalized," I read. Digitalized? Of course, given digitalis. How did you calculate the correct dose?

I read on, afraid to leave the old woman and equally afraid to stay with her. I took her pulse. It was weak and rapid. She coughed and a small amount of froth appeared on her lips. Anxiously I wiped it away with a towel.

With enormous relief I heard the intern's footsteps finally turning into the room. "You're right," he said as soon as he saw her. "She's in trouble."

He listened to her heart and lungs and then eased her down and palpated her abdomen. "Here, feel this," he said as he placed my hand over her abdomen. "That's an enlarged liver from heart failure." He lifted the sheet, exposing her legs, and pressed his thumb into her swollen ankle. His thumb left a deep impression that lasted for a long time. "Edema," he said. "Another sign of heart failure."

He replaced the sheet over her legs. "What we're going to do is give her digitalis. It strengthens the heart and makes it beat more strongly. It's one of the most ancient drugs there is. Witches used foxglove, which is *Digitalis purpurea,* to cure dropsy—the old term for edema. When dropsy was due to heart failure, they must have had some success. Now we're more sophisticated, but the drug is the same." As I listened to him talk, I began to feel my panic subside.

He wheeled the EKG machine nearer the old woman's bed and attached the small metal electrodes to her wrists and ankles. She didn't even open her eyes. All her energy seemed to be concentrated on breathing. The machine hummed as he ran out a strip of paper with the EKG reading on it.

A nurse came into the room and stood silently behind us. "I want a milligram of digitalis—the Cedilanid preparation—drawn up in a syringe right now," he told her without looking up from the EKG.

"An overdose of digitalis can be very toxic," he said. "That's one of the reasons it's usually given orally or by intramuscular injection. But it works faster if you give it intravenously, and we don't have much time with this woman. Have you ever started an IV?"

"No."

"Well, here's your chance," he said.

If he saw that I was alarmed, he didn't show it. He was trying to teach me by offering me an opportunity to practice on a real patient.

"I've only drawn blood once," I stammered, "and that was on my lab partner. I'm afraid I might have to stick her several times. I haven't had enough practice yet."

"You've got to learn sometime," he said. "Here." He handed me a needle and a syringe. "After you start the IV you can inject the digitalis."

I tried to steady my hands. Holding my breath, I jabbed the needle into one of her distended veins. She didn't even wince as the needle perforated her skin.

"Good," the intern said. "See how easy it is? Now connect the IV tubing to the needle. Tape it down carefully. Inject the digitalis slowly."

I did that, and when I finished, I put down the syringe with relief. The intern checked her EKG again and then turned to go. "Why don't you stay with her," he said. "She's not the usual patient for physical diagnosis, but it will be a good experience for you. I'll be back soon."

I followed him out of the room and found a chair, which I carried back and put near the bed. I sat down and opened my textbook again to the chapter on heart failure. Everything happening now to this old woman was exactly as described in the book. I looked from the book to her. I lifted the edge of the sheet and looked at her swollen feet. I thought of the hours she must have spent standing on those feet, holding a pose for an artist. I imagined her stepping down from the platform on which he had placed her and walking gracefully to the easel to look at her picture. I put my hand gently on her foot. It felt cool. I glanced at her face and saw that her forehead was wet from large drops of sweat. I stood up and patted it dry with a bit of gauze bandage that had been lying on the nightstand.

"Are you all right?" I asked.

"Yes," she gasped. "Don't leave me."

Evening approached. My classmates had left hours ago. I decided I'd stay with her at least for a little while.

"I'll be right here," I said.

She moved her hand as if searching for mine. I reached out and took her hand. I could easily sit and hold her hand and read my book at the same time. And so I sat for more than an hour. I was trying to study about heart disease with all my concentration, but I found myself reading the same sentences over and over again. The only sounds in the room were the turning of the pages of my book and her labored breathing. Every once in a while she coughed a little and then seemed to sleep. But the pressure she kept on my hand made me realize she was not asleep at all.

The intern came into the room again, looked at her and shook his head. "We'd better give her some more oxygen." He turned up the flow valve on the tank. "Do you want to come down to the dining room with me and get some supper?"

The old woman's hand tightened perceptibly on mine. "No," I said. "Thanks, I'm not hungry." He nodded and left.

Another hour passed. I finally finished reading the chapter on heart disease. I wondered if I should try to examine her and look for the signs I'd just been reading about. But it seemed as if it would be wrong to disturb her. Ninety-two, I thought, and dying alone in a strange hospital. Did she realize what was happening? She hadn't protested when her nieces left. But then what could she possibly have said?

I studied her face, looking for traces of the beauty that had once been there. I longed to ask her about her life. What had it been like to be a celebrated artist's model so long ago?

Occasionally she would open her eyes and look at me for a minute before closing them again. I knew from the way she clung to my hand that I had to stay. I picked up my textbook and stared at the page. Something in the sound of her breathing made me put down the book and look closely at her face. She opened her eyes and met mine directly. She managed a faint smile. What could she be thinking? Was she frightened? What did death feel like as it approached? Could she possibly tell me?

Taking off her oxygen mask, I bent close to her and asked softly, "What is it like?" I wanted her to have the chance to say something before she died.

For a minute it seemed she hadn't heard me. Then in a

weak voice full of sadness, she said, "It's hard. Very hard."

I sat beside her for hours, holding her hand and looking at the pages of my book. I couldn't think of anything more to say, and she never spoke another word. I was gripped by the loneliness of her dying. If I hadn't been there that evening, she wouldn't even have had a stranger with her. Certainly her long life deserved something better. All at once I became aware that the room was completely quiet. Her hand still held mine but not as tightly. Tensely I held my breath as I evaluated the silence. She wasn't breathing. I stood up quickly and bent over her. A rattle sounded deep in her throat, and her head sagged to one side.

Suddenly my heart beat rapidly. Calm as I had been for the last few hours, I was now terribly shaken. I knew there was nothing to be done, but I felt I had to do something. I ran out of the room. I looked for the intern but couldn't find him. I saw a nurse and rushed to her.

"My patient just died," I said.

"You must be the student who stayed with the ninety-two-year-old lady," she said. "What time did it happen?"

"A few minutes ago."

She looked at her watch. "We'll call it seven forty-five." She made a note on a pad. "But you can't declare her dead. I'll have to get the intern."

I waited outside and tried not to look upset when the intern arrived.

"I can't find her pulse," I told him. "I think she's dead."

"I've been expecting that ever since I saw her EKG," he said. "Her heart was too far gone. Come on," he picked up an ophthalmoscope, "I'll show you how to declare some-one dead."

Reentering the room we walked up to the body on the bed. He lifted the old woman's limp hand and let it fall back on the bed. "Not being able to feel a pulse or see any sign of respiration is not good enough. People without a percepti-ble heartbeat or respirations can be in a coma and look dead when they're not. There's only one sure way to tell. You have to examine the retina of her eye."

He opened one of her eyelids. The dead eye stared back without expression.

"Look into her eye," he said, handing me the ophthal-moscope with its light on. "Through the pupil and lens you can see the smallest blood vessels on the retina. When the heart stops beating and the blood no longer flows, the blood cells clump together in little groups separated by serum. In the tiny vessels of the eyes this alternation of clear serum and red blood cells looks like a row of boxcars standing on a train track. Do you see what I mean?"

Yes, I saw what he meant, and I put down the ophthal-moscope.

"It was good that you could stay with her," he said, walking with me to the door. "Don't look so depressed. I was upset, too, when my first patient died. But you've got to learn to take it in stride and not let it interfere with the rest of your work. Or else you'd better go into something like dermatology where people rarely die."

I couldn't bring myself to look back at the old woman as I left the room. I'd decided to go to the library and study where I'd be among other people. I didn't want to be alone in my dormitory room. I didn't want to think about my first death.

two

Ingmar Wollenstrum

But I did think about the old woman who died in the lonely hospital room. The sympathetic intern had made me acutely aware that death was something I would have to get used to. I realized that what had disturbed me so much was not really her death but the way in which it had taken place. I remembered again the pressure of her hand on mine. She had been frightened. And her fear and my inability to do anything for her had frightened me.

Then I remembered that once before I had experienced these same emotions about death—the same distress, helplessness, fear—all mixed together. It had been over my anatomy cadaver.

When I discovered I was going to spend part of my second year of medical school dissecting a body in anatomy, I tried to convince myself that it wouldn't be so bad. But I had strong feelings of uneasiness.

The day anatomy class began, I stood outside the lab with the other medical students waiting for the locked door to be opened. I could tell from the tension in the group that I was not the only apprehensive one. There was a lot of talking and joking, but it sounded strained. Our professor arrived and unlocked the door, and suddenly it was so silent I could hear the person next to me breathing. Slowly we funneled inside. The anatomy lab was a large room with a row of windows on one side and blackboards on the other. Twelve shiny steel tables carefully spaced several feet apart took up the whole room. On each table a stiff and cold body lay on its back.

"Pick any one you want," the professor said. "It will be yours for the rest of the year." What struck me was how very different each body was. Some were bald, some were fat and one was missing a leg. Even in death each retained its individuality.

The smell of formaldehyde was overpowering. I felt as if I was going to be sick, and I closed my eyes for a minute to shut out the scene. I can't stand this, I thought. I'll never get used to it. But if I want to be a doctor I'll have to.

I looked at the student next to me and saw his Adam's apple move as he swallowed hard. I put on as calm a face as I could muster and pretended I wasn't bothered at all by the sight of the corpses.

Students walked from table to table inspecting the cadavers. I stopped near a table with a woman's body on it. She was more shocking for me to look at than the male cadavers, and I could feel my stomach turn again.

"No, no, don't stop there," a student behind me said. "You don't want a female—too much fat on them. Pick a lean one."

The sight of that roomful of dead bodies was grim and

disturbing. I'd always thought that everyone had a dignity in death. Here was the shocking realization that for these dead people not a shred of dignity remained. Nothing. Naked and unwanted, they were being sized up as to how good a specimen they would be.

"Will you tell us what they died from?" one student asked.

"No, that's for you to find out," the professor answered. "No medical history comes with them—not even a name."

I selected a table in the far corner of the room near the window, without even a glance at the cadaver. It was the window I was after. I wanted to be able to open it and let in some fresh air. The body on this table had, through an oversight, an identification tag still tied around its big toe. The crumpled yellow tag was the kind used to ship freight. I touched it and then read it. "Ingmar Wollenstrum, 56." I glanced about the room. No other body seemed to have a tag. No one was looking my way. As if it were forbidden, I surreptitiously untied the tag and slipped it into my pocket. I felt I had been entrusted with Ingmar Wollenstrum's identity. I was the last person ever to know his name.

As I stood fingering the tag in my pocket, the man who had advised me to get a lean cadaver walked by. "I see you've found a skinny one," he said, clapping me on the shoulder. "Good girl."

Was Ingmar skinny? I made myself look carefully at my cadaver. He'd been tall and well built. He had a tattoo on one of his muscular arms. I put my finger on his arm and touched the tattoo. The colors had not faded, although his skin was tough from formaldehyde. The tattoo was of the little mermaid who sits on a rock in the harbor of Copenhagen looking out to sea.

He must have been a Danish sailor, I thought. How had

he come to this end—an unknown corpse in a strange country, his name on a freight tag?

Throughout the year as I sat dissecting him, I tried not to imagine Ingmar's life, but I pictured him strong and vital, looking at the sun from the deck of a ship, hauling in a rope, feeling the spray of the ocean. I memorized the exposed tendons of his hand and wondered in what barroom brawls it had been, what women it had caressed. I wondered how Ingmar had died, and where. Had someone been with him?

The smell of formaldehyde, which was now his smell, pervaded my clothes and hair and was with me all that year. I dreamed about Ingmar many times. He was always very much alive in the dreams. I never told this to my fellow students. We didn't talk about the effect the cadavers had on us; nor did we talk about death. But being around the cadavers changed our behavior. At the start of the year the anatomy room was very quiet. We worked diligently and spoke in subdued voices. "The body is the temple of the soul," our professor told us. "Treat it with respect."

As time passed, however, our subconscious anxieties had to find an outlet. We became rowdy and raucous. More and more obscenity replaced our usual language, and dirty jokes were traded from table to table. Many cadavers were given names. There was a Casanova and a Valentino, and the female cadaver I had not chosen was called Toots. I was as bad as the rest, but I never gave Ingmar a nickname nor did I ever say his name aloud.

You can get used to just about anything—and I did. We all did. No one passed out the first day; no one dropped out of medical school. We masked our emotions and curbed our imaginations in favor of scientific interest. It was a sink-or-swim introduction to shutting off our feelings. I was so successful at it that until the old woman's death I seldom even thought of Ingmar except to be grateful that he was the best and easiest cadaver in the room to dissect. I never did find out what he died from.

○   ○   ○

During those first two years of medical school, the encounters with the old woman and Ingmar were really the only incidents that greatly disturbed me. The last two years I spent on hospital wards. I rotated through all the services and learned how to take a complete history and do a thorough physical examination. I knew the right questions to ask. The one question I did not ask my patients was how they felt about their illnesses. What was it doing to them emotionally to be sick or close to death?

Since I was on each service for several months, I had a chance to follow my patients from their admission to discharge. Every day I talked to them, examined them, wrote notes in their charts and read up on the medicines that the interns had ordered. Every day on rounds the other students and I discussed the patients and their courses with our attending physician. When therapy was going well, the case presentation was always done at the patient's bedside. But if the patient had a fatal disease we were careful never to talk about it in front of him. On rounds we would move quickly past his bed, or if he was in a private room, we would not enter at all.

"Let's not disturb him," our professor said about a man with advanced cancer. "The patient is understandably depressed. There is no need for us to intrude on his privacy."

We'd stand outside and discuss his illness away from him.

The closer a patient came to dying, the more we talked about him as a set of variously diseased and failing organs which we must keep functioning with our skills. The disease process and how to arrest it took priority over the whole human being. By the time we had finished discussing each organ system—cardiac output, lung function, liver function, kidneys, hematologic evaluations and the state of his elec- trolytes—it was easy to ignore what the patient was feeling. In our minds we fragmented the patient in order to under- stand what was happening. I don't think we ever thought of a terminally ill case as a total person.

We believed we passed by patients' beds and rooms out of feelings of decency. We sincerely thought we were being considerate by not intruding when there was nothing more we could do. This made me uneasy and sad, but it never occurred to me that dying people might appreciate being disturbed by any one of us—that they might want to hold onto anything that could temporarily interrupt their deep- ening estrangement from life. When death became unavoid- able, it was always a relief to find that the dying patient was religious; we could turn the person over to a priest, who would fill a need that we knew we could not.

I learned in my student years to associate death with failure. All of us were being trained to use every bit of our intelligence, our time and our energy to prevent death. If I took a good enough history, did a careful enough physical examination, made the proper diagnosis early, used the cor- rect therapy, then my patient should do well. When the instructor said to me, "That was a nice diagnosis you made," I walked on air.

But if a patient died, I had very different feelings. Postmortem conferences, an important part of medical training, were held after each death to analyze the treat- ment and see if anything better could have been done. Each time a patient died, we were required to go to the pathology department and watch the autopsy. Sometimes it revealed medical conditions that had not even been suspected when the person was alive. I remember when a patient who had died of a brain tumor was found also to have had a large gastric ulcer that had escaped diagnosis.

"You mean you didn't suspect this ulcer?" the pathologist asked the student whose case it was. Of course the student felt awful, but he wouldn't make this kind of mistake again, and neither would I.

No wonder we went over and over each case that resulted in death. I would agonize if the patient was mine, wondering if I might somehow have altered what had happened. And in accepting that a patient's death could be due to my failure, I was adding an overlay of guilt to my already unsettled feelings about death.

o   o   o

Obstetrics came in the third year of medical school. My first day on that service I admitted a young woman in active labor. She was perfectly healthy, and her pregnancy was at term. After examining her, I listened long and hard with the fetoscope over her huge abdomen for the fetal heartbeat but couldn't hear it. I assumed this was my inexperience and called the obstetrical resident.

He took the fetoscope from me, listened briefly and then asked the woman, "When was the last time you felt the baby move?"

"Not for several days," she answered.

He examined her and listened carefully again. Then he shook his head and said, "I can't hear the heartbeat either. We're going to put you to sleep and deliver the baby right now."

The woman's face contorted with pain. "My baby's dead, isn't it?"

"I'm sorry," he said. He tried briefly to comfort her and then led me out of the room. "Go scrub and put on a sterile gown. I'll have her moved to the delivery room and call the anesthesiologist. This will be a good chance for you to learn how to deliver a baby."

When I entered the delivery room, the woman had already been lightly anesthetized, and the resident was piacing drapes over her legs. He motioned to me to sit on a stool in front of the woman's widely spread legs and then stood directly behind me.

"Just pretend it's the mannequin you're working with," he said. "Control the delivery. Slowly now. You don't want the mother to tear. Make your cut here for the episiotomy." He handed me a pair of sterile scissors. "Careful. Don't let the baby's head pop out too suddenly. That could cause bleeding into its brain if it were alive. That's it. Easy. Deliver the anterior shoulder. Now the other one. No, no, don't pull the baby—let her push it out. Good," he said as the pale, limp baby slid into my hands.

Its delicate skin was coming off in sheets. Every place I touched, a layer of skin peeled off.

"It looks as if it's been dead for at least three days," the resident said. "If its mother had come in then, maybe we could have saved it. Now clamp and cut the umbilical cord. Then deliver the placenta. You'll have to stand up to do that." He took the dead baby from me and put it aside on a table. Then he said, "When we're done, I want you to go to pathology and watch the postmortem exam on the baby. Let me know if they find any reason for its death."

In the autopsy room the pathologist weighed the baby, measured it and asked me its history.

"There really is none," I said. "The mother is healthy and had prenatal care. She said the baby stopped kicking a few days ago." I looked at the baby's tiny form, which its mother had never seen. It was difficult to conceal how much the sight of it upset me.

The autopsy did not disclose the cause of death. One

possibility, the pathologist told me, was that the baby had compressed its umbilical cord and cut off its own blood supply.

I returned to the obstetrical ward and told this to the resident. The mother had been moved from the delivery room, and I was not present when he spoke to her. I wondered what he said and how she reacted. It must be so terribly hard to accept a death that has no known cause, I thought.

I realized that I had suppressed my strongest emotions when I had delivered the dead baby and watched its autopsy. It didn't occur to me then that I was learning to ignore those emotions in order to distance myself from thoughts of death that were frightening to me. But the same emotional discipline that had allowed me to face my cadaver day after day, to cut into his most private parts, to hold his very brain in my hands, to think of him as a group of organs, not as a human being, was teaching me to assume tight control over all my feelings.

○   ○   ○

My second delivery on the obstetrical service started out as badly as the first one. The mother had just arrived at the hospital and was already in hard labor. The nurse helped her off with her street clothes and into bed. She put a thermometer in the woman's mouth and a blood-pressure cuff around her arm.

While I waited I listened for the fetal heartbeat. I could not hear it. I took the thermometer out of her mouth and asked, "When did you last feel your baby move?"

"A few minutes ago," the woman answered.

"When is it due?"

"Not for two months," she said between pains. "But it's coming now. I know it is."

She turned on her side, arched her back and rubbed it with one of her hands. The nurse ran out of the room to get the resident. The woman screamed and started to deliver. I saw the bulging bag of waters protrude from between her legs. Dropping the fetoscope and pulling on a pair of sterile gloves, I delivered the baby, still completely enclosed in its amniotic membranes. With shaking hands I pulled at the membranes. There was a gush of fluid as the caul came away from the baby's face, and to my relief, the tiny premature infant breathed. I was patting it dry with a towel when the resident arrived.

"You seem to have done fine without me," he said. "Take the baby to the premie nursery quickly before he gets cold." Only then did I notice that the baby was a boy.

I wrapped him in a warm blanket and showed him to his mother. "He's little," I said, "but very much alive. After all, he was born with a caul. That's supposed to mean great luck, so he should do well."

Later the pediatric intern told me the baby only weighed two and a half pounds. But despite his size he thrived, and I felt real joy whenever I went to the premature unit to see how well he was doing.

o   o   o

I finished my fourth year of medical school on the pediatric service. Late one night two worried parents brought in their crying baby. The infant had a temperature of 105 degrees. His little ribs stood out with each breath he took, and when I listened to his chest with my stethoscope, I knew he had pneumonia. I admitted him to the hospital, drew a blood culture, got a chest X-ray and started an intravenous infusion for the antibiotics that would cure him.

In the waiting room I reassured the parents that the therapy had been started and explained the illness to them.

"Everything is under control now, and I'd expect him to do well."

"I can tell you don't remember us," said the mother, "but this is the second time you've told me he'd do well."

I looked puzzled.

"Remember a two-and-a-half-pound premie who was born with a caul that you delivered last year? You said those very same words after he was born—and you were right."

I smiled. This was what I loved. Babies that lived. Children who recovered from terrible diseases because of prompt treatment. Those who were less disturbed by terminal illnesses or by babies who died before birth—let them become internists and obstetricians. Caring for dying patients was the part of medicine I hated. Life and nature were on the side of the pediatrician. I decided I'd rather use my energy to add seventy years to the life of a baby who was sick than use all my medical efforts to add a little more time to the life of an old person who was going to succumb in spite of everything that could be done.

Without hesitancy I applied for a pediatric internship, and I was accepted.

I began to pack my textbooks into boxes and my clothes into suitcases for the move from the medical-school dormitory to the hospital house-staff residence. Late one night I opened a dresser drawer in my bedroom to empty it. Under the tissue paper that lined its bottom something yellow caught my eye. I lifted the paper and found the tag I'd removed from Ingmar's toe. It had lain there for almost three years, just where I'd shoved it after I'd brought it home from the anatomy lab.

How much I've changed, I thought, looking at the tag in my hand. What was I to do with it, this stubborn remembrance of a dismembered man? The tag still had a faint odor of formaldehyde. I held it closer to my nose and the almost forgotten odor brought back all my unsettled and buried feelings about death, all the revulsion and helplessness. Suddenly I became angry at myself. I didn't need any reminders of death. Without looking at the tag, without seeing the name Ingmar Wollenstrum again, I carried it down to the basement and dropped it into the incinerator.

The iron door of the incinerator slammed shut with finality. I walked back to my packing well aware of what my gesture meant. I was leaving death behind. I was going to be a pediatrician.

three

Laura

Sometimes I cannot remember Laura's last name, but whenever I take care of a patient who is dying, such vivid memories of her come to me that I imagine her sitting in the hospital bed in place of my real patient. It always gives me a terrible shock. The vision looks exactly as Laura did— propped up on pillows, gasping for breath, dying alone, shut off from everyone except one inexperienced doctor, me.

I've never shaken off the legacy of unhappiness her death left with me, so maybe it's not that strange that occasionally I block out her name.

o   o   o

The hospital in New York at which I was doing a pediatric residency in 1962 had a reciprocal arrangement with a large cancer center. They rotated one of their residents through the cancer hospital every two months. The cancer hospital thus got a resident to start the intravenous infusions, write daily notes on what was happening to each patient and do all the work that had to be done to care for very sick patients. The residents were supervised and taught about cancer and its complications by research doctors on the staff of the center.

I hadn't found the idea of spending two months in the cancer hospital appealing. Several other residents from our hospital preceded me. During the months they served in the cancer hospital we rarely saw them, although the two hospitals were just across the street from each other. When they came to teaching rounds, or when you passed one in the residence hall where we all lived, you couldn't fail to notice that they looked more worn out than the rest of us. They had all lost weight; they all looked depressed. Their humor disappeared. Some who had been the life of the party before that rotation were no longer a delight to be around during our free time. The most positive statement made about that rotation was "It's really quite an experience." Nobody looked forward to it, and I was no exception.

The night before I was to begin on that service, I went to the cancer hospital and had dinner with Mike, the resident whose place I was to take.

"You'll be taking over my cases," he said. "And they're so complicated and some of them so critically ill that unless you put in four or five hours tonight getting to know them, tomorrow will be a nightmare for you—as well as for them."

We had dinner in the hospital dining room. Most hospital cafeterias for the house staff leave a lot to be desired, but the one at the cancer hospital was elegant. The food was delicious, and the tables were attractively set. The lighting was low, and large green palms in pots lent a solid Victorian air to the room that was very soothing.

"I never imagined a hospital could have food like this,"

I said as I enjoyed lobster thermidor. "How come you've gotten so thin, Mike?"

Mike looked at me speculatively. "Enjoy the food tonight," he said. "It'll probably be the last time you do. I used to come here every chance I could, just to get away from the ward, but I lost my appetite the first week. I can't wait to get back to our crummy cafeteria with its Formica tables and spaghetti, far away from what goes on in this place. I want to be back where patients survive most of the time. I've forgotten what it's like to watch a child walk out of the hospital cured. Oh, I shouldn't complain and prejudice you," he said grimly. "You may not find it as depressing as I did."

Mike lit a cigarette, took a deep drag and ground it out in his unfinished dinner. "C'mon," he said, abruptly standing up, "let's go upstairs and get started." He put his hands in his pockets as we walked down the hall. "You see, it's not just that the children have cancer, but the drugs that are used—Christ, they're as bad as the disease. You inject the chemotherapy drugs and a few hours later your patient is vomiting blood or screaming with cramps. The staff doctors who decide on the chemotherapy aren't here in the middle of the night, so you've got to deal with it. You won't find much about what you're going to see in any of the textbooks. It's all too new. Oh, it's a learning experience, all right." His bitterness took my breath away.

"What drugs do you use?" I asked.

"Except for the steroids, which make a patient feel good, they're all cellular poisons. The idea is to find the combination of drugs or the dose that will kill the cancer without killing the patient, too. Unfortunately the side effects of the drugs are sometimes horrendous. One little girl who was my patient went into kidney failure and died from that, although her cancer would have killed her anyway.

But what really upsets me about this place is that no one ever gives up and just tries to make the child comfortable. There's always one more drug to be used, even when it's obvious that the child can't live much longer."

Mike was so angry his face was pale. I was shocked. After a silence during which he collected himself, he said, "You'll have a chance to see what I'm talking about. It's interesting as far as basic physiology is concerned. But that's not why I went into pediatrics. Maybe you'll get more out of it than I did."

We took the elevator to the pediatric ward.

"There are fifty patients on this floor," Mike said. "We have them divided up between us. There are four residents from different hospitals working here. Those I've worked with are nice guys, bright, well trained, willing to help when I had too much to handle and good to talk with. I hope you're as lucky. You'll be responsible for about ten patients. It's hard not to get terribly fond of them, but don't let yourself. Every one of them is probably going to die."

I followed Mike out of the elevator onto the ward. We sat down at the nursing station in front of a large rack full of charts.

"Actually," he said, "sometimes the drugs seem to work. The cancer recedes, and maybe you'll even get a cure. That's what it's all about. But if I had a child with leukemia, I'd only treat him with steroids and blood transfusions and keep him home until he was ready to die."

Mike handed me a list with my patient's names, ages and diagnoses. The youngest was only six months old and had a kidney tumor. The oldest was twelve.

After we read the charts, Mike took me around the ward to meet my new patients. It was about 7:00 P.M. Most of them were lying awake in their beds waiting for night-time medicines or narcotics. At the door of one of the rooms Mike hesitated and then passed it by.

"Laura's in there," he said. "You don't have to bother about her. She's a private patient of Dr. Lassen, one of the staff men. Occasionally there are private patients here. We start their IVs, but their doctors write all the orders. Laura's got osteogenic sarcoma. It's pretty far gone. In fact, she's dying."

"What's my responsibility if she dies when I'm on call?" I asked.

"Not much. Lassen may come in, since she's his patient. Her parents are here most the time. If Lassen doesn't come in, you'll have to be the one to pronounce her dead, and you should put a final note on her chart. But don't worry about her. You'll have enough to do to keep you busy."

After Mike left, I went to the doctors' lounge and poured myself a cup of coffee. There were some stale donuts on a plate near a stack of much-read journals. I took a donut and a cup of coffee back to the nursing station and sat down to go over my charts again. I made notes on things to look up so that in the morning I would know what I was talking about.

Laura's chart was stacked in the chart rack. I picked it up and read it, and later I learned the background to her story.

o   o   o

The night I met Laura was two weeks before what would have been her fifteenth birthday. Six months earlier she had been an aspiring ballet student. One afternoon at practice she banged her leg. A large bruise formed on it. She limped a bit for a few days, but thought little of the injury.

Dancing had conditioned her to the pain of cramped toes and aching muscles. However, two weeks later the bruise was even larger and had turned an ugly purple. Laura showed it to her mother, who took her at once to see a doctor.

The doctor examined Laura. He told her nothing but ordered X-rays of the leg. When the X-rays came back, he asked Laura to leave the room. He put the X-ray on a view box and showed it to her mother.

"Look," he said, "here under the bruised area the bone is abnormal. You can see it looks as if it's been eaten away."

He didn't tell them what he suspected. He said Laura had to be seen by a bone specialist. That appointment was made for a week later.

She returned to school but not to ballet practice. She was heartsore because a recital was coming up. Still, she had confidence her leg would heal with time. It simply had to.

Laura and her mother kept the appointment with the bone specialist. The young dancer sat confidently on his examining-room table and said, "I've got to get back to practice soon," and she smiled what she hoped was her most appealing smile.

The doctor ran a finger over the bruise on her leg and said, "Hmmm." Then he took her mother into another office and closed the door. To Laura's mother he said bluntly, "I think there's cancer in the bone. I don't take care of that. It should be treated in a special cancer center. I'd like you to take her to Dr. Lassen. He's on the staff of the best cancer center in this area. It's in New York, only fifty miles away."

"What—I mean—what should I say to Laura?" asked her mother, so shocked she couldn't even think of any medical questions at the moment.

"Oh, I wouldn't say anything to her yet," he said. "After all, we don't know what type of tumor it is. Wait until more information is in." He rose from behind his desk and showed her to the door.

Laura and her mother went home and packed a small suitcase. Although Laura was quite scared, she kept her fear from her mother because she didn't want to upset her. Her mother couldn't sleep at all at night, but she took the advice she'd been given and didn't tell Laura what had been said.

o   o   o

Dr. Lassen was a tall, soft-spoken man with a Clark Gable–type mustache. Laura thought him marvelously handsome and felt for a minute as if she were a heroine in a movie. Surely nothing could be terribly wrong with her leg. Dr. Lassen would take care of her, and everything would come out all right.

In his New York office he examined her and looked carefully at the ugly bruise on her leg and then at the X-rays. That finished, he ushered her mother out of the examining room and into another office. Laura's anxiety rose as she was left behind. Always Mother, she thought. Why would none of the doctors let her hear what they had to say?

"I'm going to admit your daughter to the hospital for a biopsy immediately," said Dr. Lassen. "We have to find out if there is a way to save that leg."

"What shall I tell Laura?" her mother asked. "She's very worried."

"Well, that's hard to say. I don't know what the diagnosis is yet. Just take her to the hospital and have her admitted. I'll talk to her later. Tell her I said she needs some tests."

o   o   o

Laura stood in the admitting room of the hospital and watched her mother fill out all the necessary forms. They asked for her age, a list of her past illnesses, what allergies she had, what she liked to eat, even what her nickname was.

She watched her mother sign a permission slip for treatment and surgery. Surgery? What surgery, she thought. A great uneasiness made her grasp her little suitcase more tightly. With a nurse guiding them, they entered an elevator and were taken to the children's ward. Because she was Dr. Lassen's patient Laura was put in a private room. She wished she could have been on the clinic ward where there were several girls to a room. She wouldn't have been so alone.

She'd brought with her a biography of the Russian ballet dancer Nijinsky. That night as she lay in bed reading it, a nurse came into the room and told her it was time to turn out the light. Laura showed her the book, opened to a picture of Nijinsky leaping through the air.

"I'm studying ballet," Laura confided. "I've been dancing since I was four years old."

The nurse patted her hand and said, "That's nice. Now put out the light. You'll need your sleep," and left the room.

Laura switched off the lamp by her bedside, but she couldn't sleep. Anxiously she longed for tomorrow when Dr. Lassen would come and tell her everything was going to be all right.

The next morning was bright and sunny. Dr. Lassen strode into her room. He even walked like Clark Gable, Laura thought admiringly.

"Laura," he said, "I'm going to put you to sleep and take a small piece of bone out of your leg. Then we'll look at that under a microscope and see what the problem is. It won't hurt, so don't worry."

Laura tossed restlessly all that night. She wasn't allowed to get out of bed or walk about. The surgery took place the following morning. When Laura awakened from anesthesia, she found her leg in a plaster cast. She felt weak and sick. A blood transfusion was running into her arm. Her mother was sitting by her side, looking pale and tense. The doctors took a large piece out of her bone, her mother told her; that was why her leg was in a cast. But she was going to be all right.

"Will I be able to dance?" Laura asked.

"Of course, dear, you'll be able to dance again," her mother said. "Now close your eyes and just try to sleep."

That afternoon Dr. Lassen told her mother the biopsy had shown a particularly malignant cancer, osteogenic sarcoma. He had removed all the cancerous tissue he could. Now Laura would have to be treated with intravenous chemotherapy to try to arrest the disease. This treatment was quite new, but there had been some good results with it.

The next morning Laura lay in bed while the intravenous chemotherapy dripped slowly into a vein in her arm. Outside the door of her room the cancer specialists discussed her therapy. It was decided that her leg should not be amputated because new X-rays showed that the cancer had spread to her lungs. They could only wait to see if the drugs would arrest the disease.

o   o   o

In Laura's chart, Dr. Lassen's neat handwriting described her day-by-day course since she'd been admitted. She'd been treated with a variety of intravenous chemotherapeutic drugs. The most recent note on her chart said, "This patient is now terminal. No further treatment is contemplated."

I checked the lab slips attached in the back of the chart. Despite frequent blood transfusions, she was very anemic. A few days ago it had been decided not to transfuse her anymore. Reading her chart was depressing. I was relieved she was not one of the patients assigned to me.

As I replaced the chart in the rack, I noticed an elderly couple enter Laura's room.

"Are grandparents allowed to visit this late at night?" I asked the nurse who was standing near me preparing medicines.

"Those are Laura's parents," she said. "They're not from this area. They've taken a room in a nearby hotel for now. They spend most of the day with her. Laura's dying, you know. She's their only child. So many children here seem to be only children. When they die, it's so upsetting. I never get used to it."

When I left the pediatric floor to go back to my room, I glanced through Laura's partially open door. Her parents were sitting in straight chairs by the foot of her bed. I couldn't see Laura.

o   o   o

I arrived on the ward early the next morning with the other new residents. The morning conference that day was a review of all X-rays taken of the children. The films were flipped onto a view box. The resident assigned to the patient recited the age of the child, what the diagnosis was, how long the disease had been present and what treatment had been given. Then the films were compared with X-rays taken weeks, months and, in a few cases, even years before.

Laura's films were put up.

"This is a private patient," said the doctor who was conducting the conference. "But let's talk about her even though she is not assigned to any of you. Her films are a classic series delineating the course of osteogenic sarcoma. These initial X-rays show the cancer in the bone and here in the lung." He pointed to irregular areas on the films. "In this next series of films taken several weeks after chemotherapy, you can see that the lung lesion is no longer visible. We were quite hopeful at this point that the chemotherapy would be effective. Unfortunately, in these subsequent films the metastatic lesions have reappeared and the cancer has progressed. In this most recent film you'll notice that her heart is now enlarged. This is not from the tumor but from anemia. She is anemic because cancer cells have replaced the normal bone marrow, so she cannot make new red blood cells. These lighter, fluffy shadows on the chest X-rays are not tumor but pulmonary edema, fluid which has accumulated in her lungs because of her strained heart. Although she has cancer she will probably die from heart failure."

Laura's X-rays were taken down, and we went on to the next case.

The morning passed for me in a welter of writing on charts, examining my new patients and trying desperately to read up on the drugs I had to inject into them, deciding who needed blood transfusions, who needed medicine to control vomiting, who needed morphine. I got howls of pain from the children if I failed to place an IV needle properly and had to stick them two or three times. I got an occasional smile when all went well.

In the afternoon when I was sitting near the chart rack writing notes, one delightful sight made me laugh for the only time that day. Two little boys came scooting down the hall, propelling themselves on the wheels of the tall IV poles from which were hung their intravenous fluids. The bottles of fluid clanked precariously. Pajamas flying and bare feet slapping the floor, one foot on the base of the pole and one foot for a pusher, the boys raced each other down the hall. The nurse chasing them didn't catch up until they had gone the entire length of the corridor. The grins on their faces as she marched them back to bed said the ride was well worth the scolding she gave them.

By suppertime I was grateful for the excuse to go to the dining room and get away from the ward. A gangly red-headed resident, who had been rushing about as much as I, joined me for dinner. We sat down, both of us absolutely exhausted.

"My God!" he said, "I've got enough reading to keep me up all night. I can't keep my own patients straight yet, let alone take care of the whole ward. I don't envy you being on call. You'll probably be up the whole night restarting IVs. One of the nurses said Laura was dying. That will keep you busy if everything else doesn't."

"Laura has a private doctor," I told him, "so I shouldn't have to do anything about her. I didn't even go into her room today. I sort of felt it would be intrusive. Who wants another strange face around when they're dying?"

"I didn't go in, either," he said, picking up a pile of books he'd set under the table. "Have a quiet night. See you tomorrow."

I dawdled over my coffee as I sat there alone, but I was restless. I stood up and slipped back into my starched white jacket and headed toward the ward, eager to get everything squared away for the night.

At night the ward had a different atmosphere. During the day there had been all sorts of activity; nurses and doctors going from room to room, parents talking to each other in the hall, children on gurneys being wheeled to the treatment room or to radiation therapy. Now I could hear my footsteps echo in the quiet corridor as I walked toward the nursing station.

Laura's parents came out of her room, probably going out for supper, I thought. I nodded to them, but they didn't see me. They walked slowly. The man held his hat in one hand and with his other supported his wife's elbow. Her shoes squeaked as she walked. The parents looked worn out and dejected.

The door to Laura's room opened again, and light from within formed a bright reflection on the corridor floor. A nurse came out. She said to me, "You're the new resident, aren't you? Laura's going to be your major problem tonight. She's having trouble breathing. I turned up the head of the bed thinking it might ease her breathing, but it doesn't seem to have helped. You'd better go in and see her."

I knew enough about nurses to realize that when one of them says, "You'd better go in and see her," that means it's urgent.

"She has a private doctor, doesn't she?" I asked.

"Yes, but he lives two hours away, and anyway, I've never seen him here at night."

Now I wished I'd paid more attention to Laura's X-rays. I tried to recall them. Hers were the ones with the large heart. What had been said at the conference? That she was in heart failure because she was so anemic, and that there was nothing more to be done for her. No transfusions. Not anything. Yes, that was Laura. I put the chart I was reading back in the rack. Taking my stethoscope out of my pocket, I entered her room.

o   o   o

Across all these years I can still feel my despair as I first looked at Laura. I had seen her X-rays, the shadows of the cancer in her, hours before I saw her. But an X-ray is an impersonal thing. Put it up, take it down, put it back into its brown paper jacket and forget it. Some of her X-rays had been taken this morning. By now everything must have gotten even worse. Her large heart, stressed beyond endurance by having to beat faster to compensate for the anemia, was failing more. Her lungs would be filling up with fluid, that is, what little lung tissue wasn't already infiltrated by the cancer. Through my mind went the treatment for heart failure. But of what use was such knowledge to me in this case?

I looked at the girl on the bed. She was bald, the result of chemotherapy. A brown wig sat crookedly on her head. She gasped with each breath. Her face was colorless, her lips dry and cracked. At least I could give her some oxygen to make her breathing a little easier. I moved closer to her. Her eyes were closed, but she stirred as if she sensed me. Through the damp material of her nightgown I could see the frantic pulsation of her heart and the movement of her ribs as she struggled for air.

"Laura," I said very softly, putting my hand on her shoulder, "I'm the new resident. I'm going to put this mask on your face so you can breathe some oxygen. It'll make you feel better."

Laura didn't open her eyes. I turned on the oxygen at its wall outlet. Carefully supporting her head, I slid the strap of the mask around the back of her neck and secured the mask over her nose and mouth. Her wig caught in the strap and slipped. Pathetically she tried to straighten the wig with a shaky hand.

I took my stethoscope and listened to her heart. Because of its enlargement it had a loud and furious murmur. Her lungs, filled with fluid, rustled like sticky cellophane with each breath.

As I stood by her bedside trying to organize my thoughts, a photograph on the nightstand caught my eye. It was of a girl in a ballet dress, standing on pointe, her arms gracefully outstretched. Could that once have been this child? There were no recognizable features except the large brown eyes, now deeply sunken and surrounded by black shadows.

I looked from the picture of the young dancer to the

dying child. I suddenly felt as if I didn't belong here. Where was the doctor who knew her, whom she trusted?

These thoughts tormented me as I watched Laura, who I was sure was going to die my first night on duty. I had so many things to do—charts to go over, orders to check, cases to be prepared for tomorrow's conference and IVs to start. Yet here I stood beside this tragic young girl. I knew some ways of perhaps relieving her struggle a bit, but at the morning conference it had been said that there was nothing more to be done.

The nurse came into the room behind me. I was worried that she would disapprove of the oxygen mask I'd put on Laura. Just what, I wondered, was the routine in this hospital when someone died?

I was relieved that the nurse said nothing. I was sure she was thinking I should be doing something more useful. She had told me earlier that three IVs needed restarting. I felt guilty just standing by Laura's bed. I picked up the edge of the bedsheet and wiped her damp forehead. As I did this I realized how inept I must seem. I could sense the nurse wondering what kind of a doctor would use a bedsheet to wipe a patient's face. Laura opened her eyes as I patted her face. She seemed to want to say something. I removed the oxygen mask and smiled at her.

"You're more comfortable now. Aren't you?" I said.

Laura kept her weary eyes directly on mine. Behind me, the nurse stirred restlessly. There was a long silence. I could hear the oxygen blowing through the mask.

"Don't try to talk, Laura," I said with a phony cheerfulness. "Save your strength. You'll feel better in the morning."

"I'm dying," said Laura. Just those two words caused her to pant.

I quickly put the oxygen mask back on her face. Thank God she closed her eyes. I felt she wanted something desperately. But what? Did she want me to agree that she was dying? Should I tell her? Of course not! I was utterly unnerved.

As I bent over her to fasten the straps of the oxygen mask, her eyes opened, and once again I saw such terror in them that I became frightened. She was looking to me to save her. I must find something to say to relieve her fear.

"Now, Laura," I said with as much confidence in my voice as I could, "you've been very sick before and you didn't die. It's no different this time. You're just short of breath. Close your eyes. You'll feel better in the morning."

The black rubber oxygen mask hid half her face. She tried to speak, but it muffled her words. She shook her head with a feeble motion. I knew she didn't trust me. I knew she realized that I was wrong, that in fact I was lying. I suddenly felt desperate to get away from that room.

Suppose I were to say to her, "Yes, Laura, you are dying." Then what? Why wasn't Dr. Lassen here? Where were her parents? I looked at my watch. Only a short time had passed since I walked into her room. It felt like half the night already. There were things I had to do on the ward. I musn't neglect the other patients for Laura.

With rising anxiety I glanced from Laura to the door. The nurse still watched me. I reached out and patted Laura's hand and left her.

The nurse followed me out of the room. "You'd better start those IVs," she said. "Mark has a brain tumor and convulses. If you don't have an intravenous line in, you'll have no way to stop the seizure."

"What shall I do about Laura?" I asked.

"I'll look in on her from time to time," she said. "Her parents should be back soon. She'll be all right by herself. But it doesn't look as if she'll last much longer."

In three-year-old Mark's room it was quiet. A dim night lamp illuminated his crib. I watched him for a few minutes before disturbing him. His arms were bruised where previous IVs had infiltrated. He slept soundly, one of his thin arms covering his eyes. As I lowered the side of his crib, he awoke with a start. Because of the brain tumor he couldn't focus his eyes, and one of them turned inward. He fixed the other on me. There was no mistaking his terror. He knew my white jacket meant he was going to be stuck with another needle.

"There, there, Mark," I said, "it's all right." I took hold of his arm gently to see where there was a decent vein. He howled and thrashed about. The nurse came into the room.

"I'll have to immobilize him for you," she said, leaning across the bed and pinning him down. "There's no point trying to calm him. He's too young to understand anything you'd say."

Anyway, what could I have said? It was going to hurt; best just to get it over with as quickly as possible. Praying that on my first attempt the needle would go into the vein, I wiped off his arm with alcohol and jabbed him and missed the vein. I tried again. This time blood flowed back into the IV tubing, and I applied tape to hold the needle in place.

"I'll tie him down so he can't reach over and pull the IV out," the nurse said. She slung long lengths of gauze about his other wrist and both ankles and tied them to the sides of the crib. Mark cried and cried and tossed his head from side to side. "He'll quiet down in a bit," she said.

I looked at the miserable child tied to the sides of the crib. Did his parents know how he slept every night? Was he going to die some night like this, tied to the sides of the crib so he wouldn't pull his IV out?

o   o   o

Laura . . . Laura.

What was going on in her room now? I turned my back

on Mark's crying and left him. The nurse who had been in
Laura's room when I gave her oxygen passed me as I paused
in the hall outside Mark's door. She carried a tray of medications.

"Laura's parents came back while you were starting
Mark's IV," she said. "They're in there with her now. Why
don't you go in and say something to them? I've got to get
these medications out."

Say something to them? Say what? Of course—the oxygen mask was new. I'd tell them why I'd put it on her. As I
started into the room, it occurred to me that I didn't know
Laura's last name. I walked back to the chart rack to get it
from there. Yes, that must be it. There was only one child
with bone cancer here, Laura Eddy.

Entering Laura's room, I saw her father standing in
front of the window, looking out. His back was to Laura's
bed. From where I stood I could see the street below. The
yellow street lamps shone softly on the pavement.

Laura's mother leaned against the wall nearest the bed,
her small figure pressed against it for support. Her hands
were clasped tightly in front of her.

There didn't seem to be much change in Laura's condition. Her eyes were shut. Her breathing was just as labored.

I don't think Mr. Eddy heard me come in. I walked
right up to him before he turned around. My first words,
which I'd hoped would sound confident, came out with a
stammer. "I'm—I'm the new resident. I gave your daughter
some oxygen because she seemed to be having trouble
breathing and I thought it would make her more comfortable."

I fingered the stethoscope in my pocket. Should I take
it out and listen to Laura's lungs and make it look as if I
were doing something? But suppose when I disturbed her
with the stethoscope, she opened her eyes and told me again

that she was dying? Suppose her parents heard that? I let go of the stethoscope. Better not to disturb her. She was quiet. Maybe she'd stay that way all night.

Both parents and I moved closer to Laura. We stood awkwardly near each other. I felt a poor substitute for Dr. Lassen. I was sure Laura's parents had the same thought.

"She seems a little more comfortable now," I said, attempting to ease the tension. Neither Mr. Eddy nor his wife responded.

"That's a beautiful picture on the nightstand. Was that Laura?" I asked.

I didn't realize what I'd said until the words were out. *Was* that Laura? I could have bitten my tongue at my use of the past tense. Mrs. Eddy looked away and nodded her head.

Laura coughed. Afraid she might choke, I removed the mask.

"I—can't—breathe," she managed to say.

I held the mask near her face so she would get some oxygen. Mr. Eddy turned back to the window and kept his attention on the street below. Mrs. Eddy left the room. I took out my stethoscope and placed it on Laura's back. I could hardly hear any air in her lungs. She was drowning in her own fluid. Was I just going to stand there and watch her strangle?

The obvious thing would be to give her a blood transfusion, since it was the anemia that was causing her heart failure. But this decision was out of my hands.

What about morphine? It was indicated for heart failure and was good for pain, too. Was Laura in pain? It didn't seem that anything actually hurt her; it was just that she couldn't get her breath. My experience with morphine was limited. I'd only seen it used once. I'd never had the chance to give it myself. Why not give her some? Maybe, I thought,

44

Dr. Lassen's already ordered it for her. Why didn't I call him and let him know what was happening?

Laura coughed again. I took the stethoscope off her back and put it into my pocket.

"I'm going to call Dr. Lassen," I said as I walked by her father.

"You do that," he replied.

Outside Laura's room her mother was crying. If I made the call from the front desk, she would hear every word I said. I couldn't possibly discuss Laura's condition with her listening. There was another phone in the doctors' lounge. I'd take Laura's chart from the rack and call from there. I picked up the chart and checked the order sheet. There was no order for morphine.

The nurse walked by to replenish her tray with more medications. There were specific times to give them out, and she was hurrying now not to get behind.

"I'm thinking of calling Dr. Lassen about Laura," I said hesitantly to her. "Is it all right to disturb him at night?"

The nurse shrugged. "He knows she's terminal. He was in to see her today. You certainly don't expect him to come back tonight, do you?"

"No," I said, feeling foolish. "But I noticed that Laura doesn't have a morphine order, and I just wondered if he wanted her to have some."

The nurse paused while pouring pills into a little medicine glass. "We've been expecting Laura to die for several days," she said. "Just remember those IVs that need starting, and also the patient in Room 11 has begun to run a fever. You'd better examine him."

"Don't worry," I said, "I'll get it all done." I took Laura's chart to the lounge. I was too tense to sit down, so I stood as I dialed Lassen's home phone number. The phone rang and rang and then was answered. I heard music in the background.

"I'd like to speak to Dr. Lassen," I said.

"Just a minute and I'll call him," a woman's voice replied.

"Dr. Lassen," I said when he came to the phone, "I'm the resident at the hospital tonight. Laura Eddy's having a lot of trouble breathing. I was wondering if there was anything you would like me to do for her."

"I can't think of anything," he said. "I saw her earlier today. There's nothing more to be done. Tell her parents I'll see them in my office tomorrow."

"What about some morphine?" I asked. "May I give her some?"

"Morphine?" he questioned. "Is she in pain?"

"No," I hesitated. "She's not exactly in pain, but she can't get her breath, and—" I added quickly, "she's very upset. Maybe some morphine would calm her a bit."

"Sure," said Dr. Lassen. "You can give her morphine. Thank you for calling. Good night."

I hung up the phone and walked back to the chart rack. The nurse was busy transcribing orders. She didn't look up at me.

"Dr. Lassen said to give Laura morphine," I told her. "I've written an order for it. If you draw it up now, I'll inject it."

"I can only do one thing at a time," she snapped. "As soon as I'm done with this, I'll get it for you."

At last she finished what she was doing and drew up the morphine and put the syringe in my hand.

I took a deep breath as I went back to Laura's room. It's never a good idea to give patients any medicine without telling them what you are doing. I didn't know how sensitive Laura might be to morphine.

"Laura," I said softly. She didn't move. "Laura," I touched her shoulder and shook it gently. Her mother and father watched. "It's the doctor again. I'm going to give you something so you'll be able to sleep more comfortably."

Laura opened her eyes briefly. She turned her head away from me. Carefully I injected the morphine. I stood by her bed for several minutes until I was confident it had done no harm. But it didn't seem to make any difference either. What had I expected? She closed her eyes. Maybe she was breathing a bit more easily. I couldn't stand there the whole night, I realized. I couldn't think of anything to say to her parents. I remembered how she had met my eyes and said, "I'm dying."

I recalled the advice given in medical school that we not become emotionally involved with patients. If you did, your judgment could lapse. You might not be able to evaluate an illness objectively. The patient and the family could lose confidence in you. If you were to do a professional job, you must maintain a professional distance.

I had to leave. I was late with the transfusion for the child who wasn't dying. But as I walked out of the room, Mrs. Eddy followed after me. It was obvious she wanted to say something.

"I must start an IV now," I said brusquely, and I was suddenly ashamed. "But I should be done in a little while," I added. "The morphine will help her sleep. I think she looks more comfortable, don't you?"

Mrs. Eddy nodded her head and managed a faint smile. "Thank you," she said. "I'd like to talk with you when you have a minute. I know how very busy you are, but—if—perhaps—" and her words faltered as she tried to hide her tears.

I felt in my pocket for the notes I'd made earlier of things that had to be done. I checked them off. I'd already started the IV on the child with the brain tumor. I was about to take care of the transfusion, which was overdue by an hour. Then there was the child with a fever. I'd better get to him soon. How long should all of this take me? At least an hour or two. There were other things, not so urgent, that had to be attended to.

The one thing not on my list was Laura.

Mrs. Eddy brushed the tears from her face. I felt awkward and embarrassed. I looked down at my list again.

"Why don't you go down the hall to the doctors' lounge? There's coffee there. I'll take care of these things as quickly as I can, and then maybe we'll have time to talk." She reached out to touch my arm, but I'd already moved away. Her arm remained outstretched toward me.

"Thank you," she said again.

Poor woman. I wondered if she'd go completely to pieces when Laura died. Should I have an injection ready to sedate her? What could she want to say to me?

For the next hour I did the things I had to do. I started an IV without difficulty on a chubby baby. I put the child with the fever on antibiotics. I wrote orders for the morning lab work on all the patients. I felt confident and pleased with my work for the first time since I'd come on duty.

I realized I hadn't thought about Laura for the past hour. I figured I needed a cup of coffee. Why not go down to the dining room and get away from the ward for a little while? Then I remembered I'd told Mrs. Eddy I'd talk with her. Should I do that now or after coffee? I'd better do it first. My confidence vanished as I walked back into Laura's room. The Eddys were now sitting near their daughter's bed. Mrs. Eddy said sympathetically as I came in, "How hard you young doctors work. I admire you so much."

"I've done everything I have to do for a while," I said. "I was just going to the dining room to get some coffee and cake. Would you like to join me?" They nodded and rose from their chairs.

We all watched Laura for a few minutes. She was very

quiet. Had she slipped into a coma? To examine her now to determine that would surely disturb her, and that was the last thing I wanted.

"I'll tell the nurse we're all going downstairs for half an hour," I said. "She can look in on Laura while we're gone."

As we walked down the long, quiet corridor to the elevator, I tried to think of something to say, but nothing came to mind. Mr. Eddy's bearing precluded any small talk. His face was absolutely expressionless. It was as if there were a space around him which no one could violate. I walked next to him but not at all near him. His body could have been made of wood. It was almost as if there were a stand-in instead of a real father. I noticed he'd removed his overcoat and was wearing a wrinkled suit. The jacket was missing several buttons. His black overshoes had dried mud on them. That must have come from the park across the street. I imagined the two of them walking back each night to the hotel room. How long had they been keeping this vigil?

Why had I invited them on my coffee break? What in the world did I think we could say to each other to make the night go any more easily for us? Us? It was Laura who was dying.

We entered the softly lit dining room. I was struck once again by how pleasant it was.

"This must be real nice for you," said Mrs. Eddy. "When you're working so hard, you've got to be able to get away for a little while and relax."

Her concern touched me. I studied her carefully. She seemed too old to me to be the mother of a fifteen-year-old. She looked at least sixty. Her gray hair was brushed back off her face. The skin on her neck was wrinkled and loose. Behind her eyeglasses her eyes were a faded blue.

We sat down and gave our order. A waiter brought coffee and cake. Mr. Eddy speared his cake mechanically and finished it before his wife and I even started ours. He burned his lips on the hot coffee, patted his mouth with a napkin and stood up. "I'm going back," he said and left.

I instantly felt better. Someone would be with Laura now.

"He's worn out," said Mrs. Eddy as we watched his departing figure. "He misses our home so much. We've got a hardware store back home, and we live above it. Luckily, some good friends were able to stay there and run the store. But I worry so about him. Laura's our only child, and although he doesn't say anything, I know her suffering has ruined him. Part of him is dying with her, and I can't help him. He's never been a person to talk much, but now he's just completely shut me out. I wish there had been some way we might have stayed at home. We could have found a doctor in our town, but then Laura wouldn't have had the chance she's had here. When we go back to that hotel room at night, I feel like a traveling salesman. I don't sleep well, but my husband just sits in a chair all night and stares out of the window." Tears filled her eyes. She took off her eyeglasses and wiped them dry and put them into her pocketbook.

I couldn't look at her. I glanced at my wristwatch. We'd been there only ten minutes. Had the watch stopped? No, the second hand was moving. I put a bite of cake in my mouth, but my mouth was so dry I had to drink the coffee in order to swallow it. There was no question about it; the dying girl, the dismal hotel room, her husband's terrible withdrawal, everything Mrs. Eddy said upset me more and more. I had a night's work ahead of me, and I'd be in tears soon if I listened to her much longer. Keep your professional detachment, I said to myself. Don't get emotionally involved. Unaware of it, I sighed as I decided to stay with her only another few minutes.

As if Mrs. Eddy could sense that decision, she put her hand on my arm. "I'm so grateful you made this time for me. I needed to talk." She rummaged in her pocketbook. She'll put her glasses back on now, I thought, and we can go back upstairs.

Instead she took out her wallet and opened it to some snapshots. "Look," she said. "I've always carried her pictures. Each time I show them to someone, all the joy of having her comes back to me. She was the most precious baby you could imagine." And there was the snapshot, a chubby little baby in a sunsuit with a bonnet half-hiding enormous brown eyes.

"I married late in life, and we wanted a baby badly. For a while it didn't look like we'd get our wish, but we did. Laura weighed six pounds and two ounces and was just perfect. I was forty-five years old," she smiled. "Why, some of my friends were grandmothers already." There were no tears now. Her features became animated as she spoke, and she looked years younger.

"The day she was first put into my arms was the most beautiful day of my entire life. I'd become the most important person in the world to someone. I was a mother. And her father—I've never seen a man as happy as he was—" her voice weakened.

I thought of the man who had just left our table, his face frozen with lonely grief, walking back to his only child, who was dying. Mrs. Eddy handed me another snapshot. This one was of her husband holding a beautiful four-year-old Laura in his arms.

I'd never realized how cruel a picture could be. If I could have jumped up and left without seeing any more, I would have. But I could see she only had two more photos. These she placed on the table. Laura graduating from junior high school and a copy of the ballet-dancer picture that stood on the nightstand in Laura's room.

"She was a beautiful dancer," Mrs. Eddy said. "She had so much talent."

This time even her mother changed tenses. "She is" had become "she was." We were all referring to Laura in the past tense.

I stood up and slipped back into my hospital jacket. Looking at my watch, I said, "I'm sorry but I must be getting back to work."

"You've no idea how good it was to be able to sit and talk to you," she said gratefully. "Everyone here is so nice, but they're all so busy. You're such a fine young doctor to take the time for me when you have so much to do."

Her words made me ache. Hadn't she noticed how uncomfortable I'd been? Talk with her? Why, I'd barely given her any of my time, and even less of myself.

I pushed the elevator button, and we stood silently beside each other while the elevator rose to Laura's floor.

Mrs. Eddy walked down the hall next to me. I stopped when we reached the chart rack and sat down. She would have to go into her daughter's room without me. I'd go in there later, but now I had to give my time to my other patients.

Time, I thought as I sat staring at the chart rack, time is the real measure of how important something is. I looked at the picture that was hanging on the wall in front of me. It was a print of a familiar old painting of a doctor a long time ago sitting by a very sick child. The child lies on the makeshift bed made up of several chairs pulled together. In the background the parents stand close together, waiting. The doctor sits next to the child on a straight chair, leaning forward, his chin in his hand. His entire attention is focused on the unconscious child. There were no antibiotics in those times. There was nothing he could really do to save the child. Why then does he sit there? Why is his very presence so overwhelmingly positive?

I shook my head at my thoughts. There was no possible way I could go in and sit at Laura's bedside. I had a whole ward to care for. I wasn't even her doctor. I toyed with my pen and started to write a drug dose on a chart. I'd better stop thinking about Laura before I made a mistake. I checked the figures I'd just written. Sure enough, there was a misplaced decimal point on the dose. That was why one shouldn't become emotionally involved.

Anxiously I put down the chart and looked around. The nurse was not in sight. I went into Laura's room. Everything seemed exactly the same. Mr. Eddy stood by the window, Mrs. Eddy by the wall. Laura lay gasping and not seeming to notice anything.

I checked the IV infusion. It was running as well as before. I looked at the flow rate of the oxygen. It hadn't changed. The mask had slipped and was crooked on her face. I wanted something to do, a needle to replace, an injection to give.

I reached over the bedside to straighten the oxygen mask. As I lifted it from her pale face, Laura opened her eyes. She looked at me without expression for a minute and then turned her head slowly and looked at her mother. Her expression changed from blankness to great longing, but just for an instant. She looked back at me and said, "I—I—" and began to cough. It scared me. What if she chokes and strangles? I felt rather than saw her mother move closer. I replaced the oxygen mask and, slipping my arm behind Laura's shoulders, I tried to hold her straight up. Her feeble coughing continued. Should I get out my stethoscope and listen to her lungs? What good would that do? I must get her parents out of the room quickly before she died.

I turned to her mother and, keeping my voice steady, I said, "Would you and your husband please step outside and send the nurse in?"

Laura opened her eyes widely as her mother left. I held the oxygen mask firmly in place. Mr. Eddy followed his wife from the room.

The nurse came in. She stood by the foot of the bed. Why had I called for her? I realized it was because I didn't know what to do. There was nothing to be done. Yet I wanted someone there with me. Laura turned her head slightly. I removed the oxygen mask. Her coughing subsided.

She moaned, "I'm dying." I held her head against my shoulder.

"Laura," I said, "don't say that."

With infinite weariness she turned her head from my face. As she closed her eyes, I saw in them an expression of deep despair. Her head slumped on my shoulder. She gave a little cough.

"Get me more morphine," I said frantically to the nurse. She turned on her heel and left the room.

I stood by the bed holding Laura to me. I wouldn't be able to give her the injection if my arms were about her. I must lay her back against the pillows.

There was so little substance to her wasted body that I could feel her rapid heartbeat against my own. Unconsciously I timed my breathing to hers. When hers paused, I held my breath. My God, I thought in a near panic, this isn't what you're supposed to be doing, holding a dying patient in your arms. Carefully I lowered Laura's frail shoulders onto the pillow. Her head flopped to one side, knocking off the oxygen mask. I straightened her head and replaced the mask.

What was taking the nurse so long? At last I heard her footsteps. I turned and reached my hand toward her for the syringe. I tried to wipe off the intravenous line with alcohol but my hands were trembling so much I dropped the alcohol pad. I pushed the needle into the tubing just the same, hoping the nurse hadn't noticed my break in sterile technique. I kept my eyes on the tubing. The morphine given, I straightened up.

The nurse stood quietly looking at me. "That won't do any good now. The child is already dead."

I looked at my wristwatch. It was ten o'clock. I'd known Laura for four hours.

I had been taught how to certify someone dead. It had been impressed upon me that one never declared a patient dead without examining the retina. But I delayed. I watched her chest, but there was no sign of breathing. I felt for her heart. There was no beat. I removed the oxygen mask and wiped the saliva from her chin. She'd closed her eyes when she turned away from me and hadn't opened them again. I picked up the ophthalmoscope and reluctantly opened one of her eyelids and looked in. Laura was truly dead.

Suddenly I realized her parents didn't know their daughter had died. I listened. There was no sound outside the door. I must call them in.

Still I delayed. I cranked down the head of the bed. It would look better if Laura was lying down. The comfort I had been unable to give her while she was alive I tried to give her body now. I arranged her bedclothes neatly. I straightened her head on the pillow. I removed the IV needle from her arm and put her arms under the sheet. I folded the sheet across her chest and smoothed it again. But she didn't look at all peaceful. She looked scared, just as she had when she was alive.

Some terrible, perhaps atavistic, instinct made me pull up the sheet and cover her face. That was better. I straightened it from either side of the bed. It hung neatly without a wrinkle.

As I walked out of the room, her parents came toward

me. "Laura just died peacefully," I said. "I was giving her a little more morphine when she quietly closed her eyes and stopped breathing."

"May I—may we—see her?" asked her mother.

"Of course," I answered and led them into the room.

We stood by the side of the bed and looked at the smooth white sheet. You could hardly tell anyone was under it.

"May I—may I see her face?" asked Laura's mother.

Shocked at myself for having pulled the sheet over Laura's face, I said, "Of course," and drew it down.

"Did she say anything?" asked her father.

"No, she just stopped breathing."

I left the room terribly upset and walked down to the lounge. I stood by the window and looked out at the glimmering lights. Outside a gentle rain had started. Cars passed and people passed. No one out there would ever know what had happened here.

I remained by the window a long time. When I finally returned to the chart rack, I saw the Eddys' backs as they walked toward the elevator, leaving. Suddenly I had the impulse to say something more to them. I quickened my steps to reach them before they got into the elevator. Just then a nurse came running out of a room and stopped me.

"Hurry," she said. "In here. Mark's having a convulsion."

four

Julie:
Death Is a Rare Occurrence

I left the hospital numb with sadness and shock at the way Laura's death had taken place. I was ashamed of my role in caring for her, and yet I didn't understand why. Indeed, I had done the best I could for her at the time. Still I wished I could have kept her from dying that night. But that was only part of the problem. The other part had to do with trying to care for her while at the same time struggling to live up to what I had subtly learned was the proper professional image, an image which I sensed was all wrong. I could neither live up to it and maintain my emotional distance nor could I break down and show my sorrow. In addition, I was ashamed of myself for worrying about my own feelings when it was Laura who had suffered. I found no way to calm my inner turmoil. I had avoided the truth Laura offered me when she twice looked at me and said she was dying. My fear obstructed her honest acceptance of death.

My first response to Laura's death was a determination not to get caught in that position again. My solution was to keep myself from getting close to or loving any of the children who were near death. I decided that other dying children in my care should be protected from any knowledge of what they were going through. And I could assure this with drugs. When other patients in the cancer hospital were dying, I sedated them so heavily that they simply slept away their last days. Not one of them ever had the chance to be frightened as Laura had been.

To my relief the parents approved of the heavy sedation. Often these parents became good friends with other parents of terminally ill children on the ward. They discussed everything, but especially the residents assigned to their children.

"I was so grateful when you became Carol's doctor," one mother told me after her daughter died. "The doctor before you never worried the way you did about her pain."

What she said sounded nice, but as I heard her words, I felt like a hypocrite. True, the sedation I ordered did prevent pain, but my main reason for sedating the children was that I did not want them to know they were dying. No one ever realized this. Many parents wrote me moving letters after their children died, but in spite of their thanks I felt that something was wrong. I was robbing the children of their last days in the name of kindness. Was it really the right thing to do?

Uneasily I asked myself, would I want that kind of care if it were my own child? Since I had no children at that time, I couldn't decide. The whole idea was too dreadful to consider.

I finished my pediatric rotation at the cancer hospital,

resolved never again to undertake treating a child with cancer. If such a case came my way, I would refer the patient to a cancer center. In that way I would be sure never to get emotionally involved with a dying child.

o   o   o

During the remaining year of my house-staff training in pediatrics, I never took the time to analyze my feelings about death. My patients occupied my days and my nights. Many of them came very close to death, but to my good fortune none of them died. The only encounter I had with death occurred once when I was on duty and another resident's patient died. I did not stay in the room with the child as I had with Laura. It was of course depressing to have to pronounce him dead and to have to talk to the parents. But I only offered a brief gesture of sympathy. They would be able to talk at length to the doctor who was in charge of their child.

o   o   o

In 1964 my residency training was over. I was invited to stay on at the hospital to study pediatric hematology, but I refused. Hematology patients often had leukemia and other fatal blood diseases.

o   o   o

An opportunity advertised in a medical journal appealed to me. It said, "Pediatrician wanted to join large multi-specialty group in California." I went to the West Coast for an interview. One look at the palm trees and California sunshine convinced me that this was where I wanted to work.

I loved my new practice, and I loved pediatrics. Advanced medical therapy, immunizations, antibiotics and ways to prevent shock had almost eliminated infant and childhood mortality. A pediatrician could practice for years without having to take care of a dying child.

I had time to get to know the families of the children who came to me, and I had the pleasure of an active in-hospital service as well. Several times a month I would be scheduled to stay at the hospital for a twelve-hour period. During this time I would oversee the care of all the pediatric patients there and take care of any pediatric emergencies that arose. Occasionally there were children with cancer or other fatal diseases in the hospital, but none of them was my patient. Years passed; my practice grew larger and my patients grew older.

o   o   o

One day when I was working in the hospital, I admitted a lovely two-year-old girl. She had been a patient of mine all her life. Indeed, Julie's family often joked that I had been her doctor before she was born, for she had been born three months prematurely, weighing less than two pounds at birth. I'd been present when she was delivered and remembered the obstetrician handing me the tiny premie who just lay in the palm of my hand. She didn't breathe, and only her slow heart rate showed that she was alive. I resuscitated her and rushed her to the intensive-care nursery, where I put her on a respirator.

The respirator kept her alive. It was seven long weeks before she was strong enough to be able to breathe without it. Antibiotics to fight an infection, blood transfusions, electrolyte solutions, intravenous feedings and a lot of time and energy were also involved in her survival.

This precarious beginning to her life and its happy outcome created a tie between her parents and me that I treasured. The fact that Julie was alive and healthy and bright was a wonderful example of how far medicine had come in its battle against death.

But on the day of her admission, I could see at a glance that Julie was very ill. Her temperature was 104 degrees. She'd been vomiting all night. She lay listlessly on the examining-room table, her usual liveliness gone. I examined her quickly. Her neck muscles had a trace of stiffness. It took only a few minutes to do a spinal tap. The fluid that dripped out of the spinal needle, which should have been clear as water, was turbid. Julie had meningitis. A few more minutes passed as I drew a blood culture, started an intravenous infusion and gave her the first of many injections of antibiotics.

The antibiotics and electrolyte solutions turned her disastrous infection into a short illness of only two weeks' duration, and I was grateful.

Every year new techniques and drugs were being discovered. More and more pediatric illnesses now had happy endings. Death in my type of practice was a most improbable event.

five

Alice

Alice Zarkoff, a pediatric nurse, had worked at our hospital for over ten years. She was a robust, lively, no-nonsense type of woman who was marvelously sensitive to the sick children's symptoms as well as to their emotional needs. I always felt comfortable when she was the nurse on duty. But I had not seen her for a number of months and made a special point of looking for her one day when I was at the hospital.

"Is Alice working the night shift?" I asked another nurse.

"No, I guess you haven't heard," she told me. "Alice came down with cancer of the throat three months ago. She's a patient in the hospital now, but she's dying."

I was shocked. "Is she conscious?"

"Yes, we nurses go down and sit with her on our breaks. She likes someone in her room. I think she's afraid to be alone. It's all happened so quickly she hasn't had any time to adjust to the idea of dying."

Alice was on a medical ward one floor below pediatrics. As I walked downstairs to her room, I thought of the times when she and I had taken care of a sick child together. I remembered Alice when she'd been working on the ward. I rarely saw her without a baby in her arms or on her hip when she was charting temperatures, answering the telephone or completing her nurse's notes.

"It takes love as well as medicine to cure a baby," she had once said to me. "They don't get well crying their hearts out in a strange crib."

I had no idea what I was going to say to her. It's far easier to walk past the room of a dying acquaintance than to go in and talk to her. But Alice was a special person, and I knew that if I were dying I'd want my friends and even my acquaintances to care enough to come and sit by me, if only for a few minutes.

I knocked on her door and opened it. Alice was sitting up in bed, looking out the window. She hadn't heard my knock, nor did she hear me as I walked in and stood next to her. She was watching the heavy fog roll in over the mountains. There would be no sunset this evening.

I stood silently watching her. The emaciated, frail woman in front of me bore no resemblance to the vibrant, competent person Alice had been three months ago.

Finally she turned her head and looked at me. She didn't say anything, just held out both hands to me. I took her hands in mine and held them. I hoped this gesture said more than "I'm sorry," more than "How unfair, how horrible." I hoped it said, "I feel your anguish."

Because of the cancer in her throat, it was difficult for Alice to speak. Her voice was hoarse, and she couldn't raise it above a whisper.

"Let me do the talking," I said. "I don't want to tire you out. You can just nod your head."

"Please," she said in a rough whisper, "I want to talk, too." She had not released my hands. Her eyes looked into mine with a desperate directness.

Suddenly I could think of nothing worth saying.

At last I said, "I can't tell you how much I miss working with you. When you were on duty and I had a sick baby in the hospital, I had such confidence in you. You gave so much more to the children than just medicines. Many of my patients asked for you years after they were out of the hospital. I want you to know it has been a rare privilege to work with you." My words sounded stilted and formal, but I didn't know how else to put them.

Alice's eyes filled with tears. "I don't want to die," she said.

Oh God, I thought. Of course she doesn't. No one does. I don't either, and certainly not like this. I saw myself someday as she was, desperately hanging on to life. What could I say to her that would not sound superficial?

As her fear transmitted itself to me and confusion clouded my thoughts, I thought of the poet John Donne. One of his most beautiful poems begins, "As virtuous men pass mildly away, / And whisper to their souls, to go, / Whilst some of their sad friends do say, / The breath goes now, and some say no,:"

How could anyone get into such an accepting state that he might whisper to his soul to go?

Alice still held my hands tightly as I sat on the edge of her bed. "Are you afraid?" I asked.

She nodded.

"So am I," I said. We sat silently.

"I'm not ready to die," she said.

I squeezed her hand gently. "Last year I had an allergic

reaction to an antibiotic and I thought I was dying. I can still remember the feeling I had then."

"What happened?" Alice asked.

"It was like a dress rehearsal for death," I began. And what a strange experience it had been.

o o o

During the pollen season in the spring I usually come down with a sinus infection. One Sunday afternoon I was at home when my sinuses began to ache. I looked in the medicine cabinet and found an antibiotic tablet and took it. About half an hour later I had a burning pain in the lower part of my chest. I told myself irritably, "You shouldn't have taken that antibiotic on an empty stomach." I drank a glass of milk and it relieved the burning, but only for a few minutes. Then the pain became so severe that I had to hold onto the kitchen table to steady myself. My chest felt as if it were being crushed. I was terrified. That's exactly what a heart attack is said to feel like.

I forced myself to walk slowly to the bedroom. "You're too young for a heart attack. You're not a man. You're not overweight." But the pain got worse, and I became more and more frightened. I felt as if a red-hot poker were being shoved inside my ribs. Then the searing pain spread down my right arm. This can't be happening, I thought. But it happens to other people every day. Why not me?

Beads of sweat broke out on my face. I picked up the telephone and called my husband, who was at a next-door-neighbor's house. "Bob, I feel horrible. Could you come home right away?"

I put down the telephone and lay down on the bed. The pain spread to my other arm. It had to be a heart attack!

My husband, who is also a doctor, rushed into the bedroom. Our teenage daughter was right behind him. He examined me quickly. "I'm going to take you to the hospital. Can you walk to the car?"

I shook my head.

"I think I'm having a heart attack."

By this time the pain was so intense that I didn't want to talk or be disturbed in any way. Bob tried to pick me up to carry me to the car, but I pushed him away. I kept thinking, "What a shame. There's so much I haven't done. I don't want to die. Not yet."

As I lay there, the pain began to recede and was replaced by a strange buzzing feeling along my arms. Then that disappeared. My arms and legs became numb. I felt as if I were floating. It wasn't unpleasant at all. It was wonderful to be free of the pain. If this is what death is like, at least it doesn't hurt. Why should I fight it? Suddenly a feeling of intense panic came over me. I must not give in to this feeling of peace. I must not go with it. I didn't want to die. I must force my eyelids open. It was the hardest thing I've ever done in my life. They felt as if they'd been sewn shut. They were simply too heavy to lift. I concentrated every bit of energy I had on just my eyelids. Finally they opened. My field of vision was constricted. I saw my husband's face contorted with worry and my daughter's stricken expression as she leaned over me. Poor Margaret, I thought dreamily, she'll have to help raise the younger children. I couldn't keep my eyelids open any longer. I stopped fighting and lost consciousness.

I came to in a speeding ambulance. I heard the shrill whine of the sirens and a voice saying, "She's got a good heartbeat now."

The ambulance driver had radioed the hospital that a Code One who might need to be resuscitated was coming in. When the ambulance pulled up to the hospital entrance, nurses and doctors with whom I had worked rushed out to steady the gurney. They quickly transported me to the section of the emergency room reserved for heart-attack victims. Their concern showed in the haste with which they attached an EKG machine to me. A cardiologist read the strip as it came out of the machine and pronounced it normal. The tension on everyone's face disappeared.

By now I was able to speak. Several doctors examined me and finally decided that I had suffered neurogenic shock because of the antibiotic I had taken. I spent the night in the hospital and was discharged the next day, none the worse for the experience.

There are two things I'll always remember from that experience—how difficult it was to force my eyelids to open and that pleasant feeling of peace when I finally decided to give up.

o　o　o

I finished the story and sat holding Alice's hands in mine.

"There's still so much I want to do," she whispered in her ruined voice.

"I know," I told her and put my arms about her. We held each other for a long time.

When we released our embrace, I recited John Donne's poem for her. "As virtuous men pass mildly away—"

She repeated the lines after me. Then I kissed her gently and said, "I'll bring you a book of his poetry tomorrow."

Alice died several days later in the hospital. Donne's poetry was on the bed beside her.

SIX

Beginning to Grow

There are twenty pediatricians in the large medical group with which I practice, and we each take hospital call about once a week. This is like being an intern again. It's a splendid way to keep current on techniques for managing emergencies and dealing with desperately ill patients. We are on duty for twelve-hour periods. At the end of this time we sign out to another colleague, discussing the course of each hospitalized patient and what the patient's private doctor has ordered. The advantages of this system are that knowledge is exchanged freely and a pediatrician is always on the scene to manage immediately any unexpected event.

At 9:00 A.M. when I came on duty at the hospital my colleague, who had been on call since 9:00 P.M. the previous night, was bleary-eyed and exhausted.

"Was it a busy night?" I asked.

"You better believe it! There was one emergency after

another, and there's a lot of croup going around. I admitted two babies with it."

We made rounds quickly because he was so tired. The two patients admitted during the night had improved and were now breathing without problems.

"We'll have to go to the intensive-care unit," he said. "Dr. Baylor has an eighteen-month-old he admitted three days ago with severe croup. She stopped breathing and convulsed and had to be placed on a respirator. She's still on it. She was in shock, and it looks as if she may be developing renal failure. You'll have to calculate her IV fluids very carefully today. Baylor is sick himself and won't be in to see her, but you can call him and let him know what the problems are."

We walked into the baby's room in the intensive-care unit. Her worried parents stood near her crib. The haggard expressions on their faces showed the terrible strain they were under.

"Unless her kidneys shut down, I don't think there will be any problems today," he said.

I sat down by the baby's bedside and read her chart. Here was another child who would surely have died without lifesaving equipment like respirators. During my career I'd seen so many near-tragedies averted by modern medicine. Now I was more confident that death rarely had a chance to win.

I went to the telephone to call Dr. Baylor. He sounded very ill. "Just keep up with everything. She's had about every complication you can have with croup. I just hope she doesn't get a bleeding ulcer from all the stress."

I went back to the nursing station to make sure we had a unit of blood already cross-matched. Then I returned and checked the baby again. There were no signs of an ulcer.

I walked out of the room to talk to her parents. They knew she was critically ill, and I merely told them that her condition seemed stable and that I had spoken with Dr. Baylor.

Two hours later I was in the emergency room when there was an urgent call for me from the intensive-care unit. I hurried to the baby's room. I could see from the doorway what had happened. The bedsheets were red with blood. The baby had had a bowel movement. As the nurse changed the diaper, blood ran out of the baby's rectum. She had developed an ulcer and was hemorrhaging.

"Open that IV up all the way," I told the nurse. "And get the blood we have cross-matched here right away."

I took the baby's blood pressure. Thank God she was not yet in shock. Maybe I could prevent that with fluids and blood.

The blood arrived in a few minutes, and the nurse hung it up. I passed a suction tube into the baby's stomach. The nurse and I worked on the baby for the next hour, running ice-cold saline into her stomach until the ulcer stopped bleeding.

During the whole episode the baby's parents had remained outside the room. But they had looked in through the doorway from time to time. I told them, "She's developed an ulcer. But the bleeding seems to have stopped now."

They nodded their heads as if they were convinced that agreeing with me would make everything come out all right. But the blood had been frightening. They knew the baby was very ill, and I could not reassure them she would not die.

As I turned to go, a group of people who had been standing in the next room also began leaving. An attractive woman, whose white coat did not hide her plaid skirt and delicate lace blouse, excused herself from the group and came toward me.

"You must be Dr. Sharkey," she said, holding out her

hand. "I'm Dr. Jennifer Conte. I've heard you paged many times today. You must have a very sick baby in there. I'm a psychologist. Maybe I can help. I work with dying patients and their families. Would you like me to talk to the baby's parents? They must be very upset."

I was quite startled by her offer. I shook my head. "This baby is not going to die. Her condition is stable. At least right now."

Jennifer smiled at my emphatic tone. "I'm good at relieving anxiety, too," she said. "No one has to be dying to need my help."

I smiled but said, "I don't think there's any need for you to talk to them."

During the course of the day I noticed that every time I went to the intensive-care unit to check the baby, her parents stiffened with tension. As long as I was not called, they must have assumed all was going well. As soon as I showed up, they grew afraid that some new complication had occurred, even though I might have come in just to check the IV fluids or look over the lab work.

Then, unfortunately, the baby began to hemorrhage again. Although I managed to stop the bleeding, it was a sign that her condition could be worsening. I grew very concerned and began reassessing what else might be done for the baby. It was then that I saw Jennifer Conte and a surgeon come into the intensive-care unit.

I walked over to Jennifer. "Do you remember those parents you offered to talk to this morning? Things aren't going well with their baby. In fact, things are going very badly, and her parents seem to cringe every time they see me."

Jennifer turned to the surgeon. "You wouldn't believe how Dr. Sharkey reacted this morning when I asked her if she'd like me to speak to those parents. She drew back as if I were the angel of death." Jennifer mimicked my expression so well that I laughed with her.

"Come on now," I protested. "I wasn't that bad. But if the baby continues to bleed, we may well be dealing with the angel of death. It might help if you did speak with her parents now."

I wasn't present during Jennifer's conversation with them, but in the evening when I entered the baby's room, I noticed that they were somewhat less tense.

Several days later the baby was recovering, and I made time to stop by and see Jennifer. She greeted me warmly.

"What did you say to the parents of that sick baby in the intensive-care unit?" I asked.

"Probably nothing that you had not said. But I had time to sit with them and explain again what you were trying to do for the baby. Parents are often reluctant to ask a doctor anything for fear it will seem as if they're questioning the treatment. You were so occupied with saving the baby that day that you certainly didn't have a minute to worry about their feelings. That's when it helps to have another person around. Parents and families don't want to get in the way of medical care, but by the same token they don't like to feel shut out. That's where I come in."

"I heard that you also talk to dying patients in the hospital," I said.

"I do," Jennifer said. "But not too many doctors will let me see their patients. They still don't understand what I'm trying to do."

"What *are* you trying to do?"

"I'm trying to get people—patients *and* doctors—to confront death humanely."

That touched a nerve. "I'm probably worse than anyone when a patient of mine is near death and there's nothing I can do. Fortunately few pediatric patients die, but I dread the thought of having to care for a child with a fatal disease. Maybe you could help me get over that."

Jennifer reached up to a bookshelf. "I've got a book I'd like you to read." It was *On Death and Dying*, by Elisabeth Kubler-Ross.

○   ○   ○

Although I was vaguely familiar with Elisabeth Kubler-Ross's name, I had not previously read her book. This most humane psychiatrist had the originality to investigate the feelings of dying patients. Like many brilliant ideas, hers seemed so simple and obvious. And kind. She pointed out that many doctors had long been avoiding the emotional needs of their dying patients, and that we were evasive when it came to handling this most important event. She felt there was a great deal we could learn from our dying patients.

As I read Dr. Kubler-Ross's book, I did not really become comfortable with the idea of death—and certainly not the idea of a child's death. A child's death would always be too great a tragedy for me to accept. But I came to understand that my need to deny death was also potentially tragic. When a doctor is so uncomfortable about death that a dying patient cannot talk to her about it, how can the patient really trust her? Certainly preventing the patient from sharing his feelings about death adds to his sense of isolation. We are indeed a sharing species. Without that, what part of life is worth living for any of us?

A doctor's unsettled feelings about death can also take the form of withholding negative diagnoses. Today it is unthinkable not to tell a patient he has cancer. But twenty years ago it was just as unthinkable to tell someone he had cancer. I remember discussions on this subject when I was in medical school. We had never been told not to tell a patient the truth. But we were told that knowing he had cancer could a rob a patient of his will to live. This was something we should consider carefully before we took that risk. The patient's life, not his death, was our concern, and we would do anything to prolong it.

If the truth be told, the patient, even if he was a child, was rarely fooled. It was the doctor, shielded by good intentions, who was protected from ever being close enough to a patient to suffer with him when he died.

In Kubler-Ross's book I found the answers to the reasons for my deep distress about the way my patients died. The feelings that I hadn't had the insight to understand at the time of Laura's death were clearly described.

The old country doctor had few weapons to cure disease and none with which to fight death. His strength was in the care and love he gave his patients, in the time he spent in their homes. Modern doctors rarely see a patient in his own home and so never know his true individuality. We are always so focused on the disease, the white blood cell count, the X-rays. There is so much to consider to cure his body that it is easy to overlook the innermost fears and needs of his soul.

I've stood before century-old paintings showing death-bed scenes and thought how different those scenes were from what usually happens now when someone dies. In those days no one kept family and friends away or asked them to step outside as the moment of death approached. In the old pictures, instead of the anonymity of a hospital room, there are always people grouped around the dying person. In times past, death was an important and recognized fact of life, something one's whole life moved toward, something one prepared for. People thought and talked about it openly. It was accepted; it was not a sign of anyone's failure.

Kubler-Ross points out that it was only when medical

science gave us such excellent ways to save lives that doctors decided dying was too terrible for family members to share. Our excuse was that the families must be protected or they would become frightfully upset, perhaps even hysterical. The truth is that I don't think we wanted anyone to witness our defeat. Our goal was to prevent death, even if just for a short time. Each day of life was a victory not to be given up lightly. The doctor fought the dying; that was his entire preoccupation, even when in all decency it was clear the battle was lost.

The tools we used in these last efforts were sometimes so grisly that relatives and friends had to be excluded. There was a period when open-heart massage was done in an attempt to revive people. This meant making a gash between the ribs, thrusting your hand into the chest and squeezing the dying heart in an attempt to stimulate it. When I was an intern, we did it all too often, even when we had little hope of saving the patient.

This way of shutting dying people off from friends and family occurred at the same time that scientific advances gave doctors the means to really cure people. It was the doctor's new ability to triumph over death that often resulted in his feelings of personal failure when he could not win. Death brought guilt to the doctor. If only he had read more, made the diagnosis sooner, used a different drug, maybe the patient would have lived.

Small wonder then that when doctors were not successful, they were threatened and depressed. Scientific excellence led doctors into their power struggle with death, and indeed many people might be dead today if it had not been for their doctors' bulldog determination to save them. But when dying is inevitable, the issue is not how to protect our feelings as doctors. It is a question of whether we want to face that reality evasively or humanely.

The dying children I had cared for were so sedated and went from life so quietly that it was impossible to tell when the moment of death had occurred except by monitoring the pulse. There had been no last words, no last declaration of love to bring peace to their parents. Drugs had robbed my dying patients of that chance and robbed their survivors, too.

These insights of Kubler-Ross brought me much closer to the truth. It was not only that it had been devastating to watch Laura lose her young life. The reason for my guilt, I realized, was that I had told her she would be better in the morning. What she had really asked of me was that I listen to her and say, perhaps, "Yes, Laura, you are dying. Don't be frightened; your parents are here." My motives may have been decent, but the result was deceitful. As I recalled the evening she died, I realized that I had been the one who was denying reality, not Laura. I had not been able to bear her words.

Elisabeth Kubler-Ross wrote, "I am convinced we do more harm by avoiding the issue than by using time and timing to sit, listen and share."

That was what I had done with Alice before she had died. I had shared her fears and told her mine. I had made no attempt to hide my sorrow. I could sense then that this had given her comfort and knew now that it had given me strength. It was all described in Kubler-Ross's book. Death was simply an unavoidable fact of life. Denial of death was an avoidable danger.

Reading *On Death and Dying* taught me a powerful lesson that I hoped would enable me to become a wiser doctor as well as a wiser human being. Yet even as I felt better prepared to help a dying patient, I still could not avoid a silent prayer that I would never be called on to do so.

seven

Peter

In December 1970 a copy of Henri Troyat's biography of Leo Tolstoy was given to me. The book included many excerpts from the diary of his remarkable wife, Sonya Tolstoy. In one of the entries she recorded that their son Petya, a beautiful baby of only fourteen months, had come down with croup. Two days later he was dead, and she wrote:

> I cannot reconcile the images of Petya living and Petya dead. They are both precious to me, but what is there in common between that being full of life, light and affection and this other, motionless, solemn and cold. He was very attached to me. Did it hur' him to leave me?

Dead from croup. I shook my head in dismay. I thought of the baby in the intensive-care unit whom I had just taken care of. She had been admitted with croup and also had a hemorrhaging ulcer. Yet she had been discharged from the hospital within ten days. Now she was as well as if nothing had happened to her. What a difference a hundred years had made in the lives of children.

o   o   o

It is not uncommon practice for the pediatricians in my group practice to see each other's patients if one of us is on hospital duty or away from the office. Phil Stevens has the office next to mine. He's a jovial man with a bushy brown beard. The children love him, and they are often very disappointed when they realize they must see me instead of him. Phil tells me I simply can't compete with his beard.

I had just arrived at the office one morning when my nurse handed me the chart of Peter Bianchi, one of Phil's patients.

"I've already put Peter in an examining room," she told me. "He has a little rash, and I thought it might be early measles."

I skimmed the chart. Peter was fifteen months old. He'd been seen only for well-baby visits. He'd had his measles vaccine. I saw from the initial note on his chart that his father was a teacher, his mother a housewife and he had no brothers or sisters. Without a fever he shouldn't be very sick.

As I entered the examining room, I saw the mother sitting in a chair holding a plump, pink-cheeked infant on her lap. Her husband was nearby, correcting exam papers.

I introduced myself. "Dr. Stevens isn't here, but I'll be glad to see Peter. Now tell me, what's the problem?"

The baby squirmed and wiggled in his mother's lap until he managed to stand up. He reached out and grabbed a handful of her long brown hair and put it into his mouth.

"I'm sure it's nothing," she said, freeing her hair and

turning him around so I could see his face, "but he's got a rash on his eyelids."

It wasn't much of a rash. The skin on his arms, legs and abdomen was perfectly clear. But on his upper eyelids there was a sprinkling of tiny red spots called petechiae. Those spots could be indicative of a bleeding tendency or a serious infection. It's a danger sign that doctors pay special attention to.

"Has he had a fever?"

"No."

"Been throwing up or acting sick?"

"No. His appetite is fine."

"When did you first notice the spots?"

"Just this morning when I got him up to change him and give him breakfast."

She wasn't worried, and at that point neither was I. The baby didn't look or act very sick.

"Let me examine all of him," I said, helping her take off his little shirt and unpin his diaper.

I went over him carefully. There were no petechiae anyplace else, no bruises, no indication of bleeding. He had no enlarged organs, and his pink-cheeked face assured me he was not anemic.

I was puzzled. I sat back to watch him for a few minutes before examining him again to see if I'd missed anything the first time. Peter played contentedly with his mother's necklace. He was an unusually handsome baby, with softly curling brown hair.

"How are you ever going to find the heart to cut his beautiful hair?" I asked, just for something to say while I observed him. I reached out to brush the curls from his face, and my fingertips touched a small lump behind his right ear. I bent his ear forward to see what I had felt.

Behind his ear were three very slightly enlarged lymph

nodes, none of them any bigger than a pea. Surrounding each node, as if you had taken a pen and outlined it individually, was a thin circle of dark blood. I'd never seen anything like it before. Thoughts raced through my mind. Those nodes must be biopsied immediately, I decided.

Phil Stevens had once told me about a four-month-old patient who had a small, hard lump on her cheek. When it was biopsied, the lump proved to be a fast-growing malignancy. The baby had died from it.

I've never figured out how such thoughts transmit themselves to parents almost before you've finished thinking them. But even as I took my hand away from the baby's head, I could see his mother's face lose color.

I brushed back the baby's hair again to show her what I had felt. "He's got some unusual lymph nodes here. I don't know what's causing them. It might be a virus or some other infection, but I do think we should find out as soon as possible. I'd like to put him in the hospital today and have one of the nodes biopsied. That's the only way we'll know what's going on."

"Could it be cancer?" Mrs. Bianchi asked me directly.

"It could be, but it could also be a lot of other things. That's why we need the biopsy. Guessing isn't good enough."

Mr. Bianchi stood up. "How soon can it be done?"

"Probably tomorrow morning," I told him. "I'll make arrangements with the surgeon, and I'll also call Dr. Stevens and let him know Peter is being admitted. I'm sure he'll meet you at the hospital if he can."

When I reached Phil on the phone, I explained about the lymph nodes and petechiae and said I had arranged for a biopsy. "The Bianchis said they'd wait for you at the hospital."

"Thanks, Frances," he said. "I'll let you know what it turns out to be."

A few days later Phil walked into my office carrying his morning cup of coffee. He sat down on the edge of my desk. "Those nodes you saw on Peter turned out to be monocytic leukemia."

"Good Lord!" I said. "It must have just started to develop. The baby didn't even look anemic when I saw him."

"He is now," Phil said grimly. "I've started him on chemotherapy and steroids, but you know how poorly that type of leukemia responds to anything."

The following week I asked Phil how the baby was doing. "Terribly," he said. "There's been no response to therapy yet."

It was almost Christmas. This part of California is as far away from anything resembling the North Pole as one could possibly get. But that's never discouraged anyone when it comes to Christmas decorations. Santa and his sleigh and reindeer are displayed everywhere, often anchored in palm trees or on a green lawn surrounded by brilliant geraniums.

Ten days after Peter had been admitted I had hospital duty for the day. There were very few patients in the hospital. All elective surgery had been put off until after Christmas, and every child who could possibly be discharged had been sent home. A Christmas tree stood near the door of the treatment room, its sparkling lights blinking off and on. Tinsel glittered from the tops of IV poles. But the bright and shiny decorations only made the ward seem sad and lonely. A hospital is the last place any child would want to spend Christmas.

I walked down the hall of the pediatric ward and saw Phil standing outside a room talking with Peter's mother, father and grandmother. They were speaking in low voices and didn't look up when I passed. The baby must be worse, I thought, and went to the chart rack to read his chart and find out what was happening.

I was right. He certainly was worse. The disease was

running an incredibly rapid course. Despite ten days of therapy none of the drugs had worked. His falling blood count had required frequent transfusions. Then two nights ago when Mrs. Bianchi was lifting Peter out of his crib, the baby had reared back suddenly and hit his head against the side rail. Because his blood clotting was so poor, this bump caused bleeding into his brain. Shortly afterward he convulsed and went into a coma. He was dying.

From the corner of my eye I saw the parents and the grandmother go into Peter's room.

Phil walked slowly over to where I was sitting. "It's really bad," he said. "I've ordered another transfusion. That should be here soon, but the damage is done. Even if the bleeding stopped, it wouldn't help his brain at this point. He probably won't last the day. His parents know exactly what's happening. They'll stay here until he dies. There's nothing for you to do, but if you have a chance maybe you could just talk to them for a while. They've already signed permission for a postmortem. Considering how miserable the course of monocytic leukemia usually is, it's probably a blessing he hit his head and is going out this easily." Phil took Peter's chart from me, made a brief note on it, shook his head unhappily and left.

o   o   o

There wasn't much work for me to do that day at the hospital. I went down to the record room and dictated some old charts and then to the emergency room to sew up a laceration on a boy who had fallen off a ladder while helping his father put Christmas lights around their home.

An emergency call about fetal distress made me run to the delivery room. I pulled a sterile gown over my clothes and rushed into the room just as the obstetrician delivered the baby. He cut the umbilical cord and handed me a limp newborn who wasn't breathing and whose heartbeat was barely perceptible. It would surely be dead in a few minutes unless it was resuscitated. Quickly I suctioned fluid out of its throat and, using an instrument to see the vocal cords, I slipped a tube into the tiny windpipe. I blew oxygen into the tube to take the place of the breathing the baby couldn't do on his own. His color turned from blue to dusky. He moved one arm feebly. I listened for the baby's heartbeat. It was picking up. His skin color became pink as his lungs started to function. A few minutes more and the baby took his first breath. The heartbeat was now normal. I pulled the tube out of his windpipe. His initial cry was soft, but the next one filled the room. Everyone relaxed; the baby was going to be all right. I dried him off, wrapped him in a warm blanket and carried him over to his mother.

"Here's the best Christmas present ever," I said, smiling.

The mother's hands trembled, and tears of relief rolled down her cheeks as she took her baby into her arms and kissed its damp hair.

I left the delivery room feeling absolutely wonderful. What a privilege it was to be a doctor.

The happy feelings left me as I returned to the pediatric ward and walked into Peter's room. Peter lay motionless in his white crib. A plastic tube to drain his stomach hung out of one nostril. An intravenous infusion ran into his arm. His breathing was shallow and irregular. His parents and grandmother sat silently near him.

My throat tightened. I went over to the bed and felt for Peter's pulse. It was weak. I opened his eyelid and saw that the pupil was greatly dilated. As I adjusted the intravenous tubing, I touched the baby's limp hand and remembered how he had held onto his mother's long hair and put it into his mouth such a short time ago.

Without meaning to I sighed, and his parents looked at me. "Would you like some coffee?" I offered. "There's always a pot in the lounge."

"That might be good," said Peter's father.

We left the room and walked slowly to the lounge. Standing for a moment by the large windows, we saw the streets full of holiday traffic and busy shoppers. Sunlight sparkled on the tops of the cars. It was all color and motion. The sight of pedestrians carrying Christmas-wrapped packages and looking so happy was almost offensive.

There wasn't much the Bianchis and I could find to talk about. We just sat, sipped our coffee and commented on the weather. Phil had told them all there was to tell. There was nothing more for me to add.

After a while I left them and went back to the nursing station to make some notes in a chart. I'd only been there a short time when the nurse came out of Peter's room. She walked over to me and put her hand on my shoulder. "I think he's dead," she whispered. "Will you come and take a look?"

I rose quietly and went into Peter's room. He didn't seem to be breathing. I touched his wrist and felt no pulse. His eyes were closed.

"Shall I call his parents?" the nurse asked.

"Wait a minute," I said. "Let's get all these tubes out of him so he looks a little more natural." I pulled the plastic tube from his nose and removed the IV from his arm. The nurse wiped his face and patted his soft hair neatly into place.

"Now call them," I told her.

The parents and the grandmother came into the room but stopped and stood quite a distance from the crib. Peter's mother alone approached the baby's body. She gently touched his hair. Holding his little head in her hands, she looked at his face for a long time. Then she said, "Oh, Peter, Peter. You were so precious to me. I had you with me for such a short time. Did it hurt you to leave me?"

Instantly I imagined Sonya Tolstoy bending over her dying son Petya.

I shut my eyelids tightly to try to stop the tears. But there was no hiding them. "I'm sorry," I said.

The mother turned her face from her dead baby to me. Tears filled her eyes and she started to sob.

Her husband put his arms around his wife and held her to him. The grandmother turned to me and took my hands in hers.

"I'm so sorry," I said again, trying to wipe away my own tears.

"Don't say anything," she said, putting her arms about me. "You don't have to say anything. It means something to us just to know you cared. Sometimes it's good to see a doctor cry."

                                                  °   °   °

Later when I considered my reaction to Peter's death, I remembered the grandmother's words. "It means something to us just to know you cared."

Never before had I let a family know how much I really did care. Why had it taken me so long to realize that it was all right?

eight

David

My office window faces a range of low mountains. In the summer they're brown and ragged, burned dry by the sun, but when the spring rains come, wild oats sprout and the hills turn a delicate green.

I remember standing by my window looking at the springtime hills just before I met David in 1971. It required an effort to turn away from them and pick up the chart of my next patient. His name was new to me, David Carver, a two and a half year old, referred to me by a general practitioner. A referral always meant a problem that wasn't simple. I took another long look at the hills and then walked toward my examining room.

Even after years of practicing pediatrics there's still a moment of exciting anticipation whenever a new patient is on the other side of an examining-room door. What will I find?

I reached for the door and opened it. The first thing I noticed was the anxiety of the parents who stood tensely in the center of the examining room. The mother held a calm little boy in her arms.

I held out my hand. "I'm Dr. Sharkey. What brings you here?"

The father extended his hand but didn't take mine. Instead he gave me a note from the referring doctor. I took it and read it quickly. Below the doctor's letterhead were onl· two words: "Hemoglobin six."

"A hemoglobin of six means David is anemic. What dic Dr. Thomas tell you?"

"Now's the time to see a pediatrician," the father answered uneasily.

"Nothing else?"

"No, nothing else."

"Has he taken care of David for a long time?"

"Ever since he was born. But David's always been perfectly well. He's had all his immunizations."

There was certainly an ominous sound to "Now's the time to see a pediatrician." I could imagine the Carvers mulling over those words while they waited to see me.

Anemia, I thought, but surely not a simple iron-deficiency anemia. Dr. Thomas would have been able to treat that himself.

"Let me examine your baby," I said. "No, don't put him down on the table. Just hold him like you're doing. He doesn't know me, and I'd rather he didn't cry."

I reached my hand toward the baby. Although I was a stranger, he didn't squirm or draw back but regarded me with grave brown eyes. There was no pink to his cheeks. Perhaps he had an inherited anemia. There is one that occurs in people of Mediterranean ancestry.

I looked at the father—tall, blond, with the thin body of

a long-distance runner and a very controlled expression on his face. He didn't look Mediterranean to me.

The mother hadn't moved a step. Short, chunky, young, probably about twenty-two, she was very quiet. The child resembled her, with straight black hair and a coppery tone to his skin. Could be Italian, I thought.

I moved my hand down the baby's chubby leg. It was splotched with bruises. I felt uneasy.

So much of life consists of naming things. Once that is done, a chain of events is set in motion that didn't exist before. True, the problem was there, but until you named it no one had to accept it. Naming is true definition. A doctor must be so careful with names.

I patted the bruised little leg. How about a diagnosis of aplastic anemia? That wasn't a nice disease, but it could be treated and not prove fatal.

One part of the baby remained to be examined before I could make even a provisional diagnosis in my mind of cancer or leukemia—a diagnosis that meant almost a death sentence for this beautiful child. I must feel his abdomen to see if his spleen was enlarged.

I unbuttoned his shirt and looked at his abdomen. It was fat like all two-year-olds'. Or was it fatter? I put my fingers on his chest. He bent his head and watched my hand. Soft skin, firm little ribs moving up and down with each breath. The pulsating of his heart was strong and normal. I ran my fingers downward. Then light as was my touch, with no wince from the baby, I felt an enlarged spleen, a harbinger of death. I had one last hope. Maybe it's not leukemia. Perhaps he has a neuroblastoma, a childhood cancer that responds well to surgery and therapy.

I looked at the parents, not at David, and said, "Your son is anemic. The bruises on his legs mean his blood clotting is disturbed. He has an enlarged spleen. Anything I tell you now would be no better than a guess. I want to put him in the hospital and have a bone-marrow test done, and maybe some X-rays. In a few hours I'll be better able to let you know what's going on. Is that all right?"

What could any parent answer? Of course it wasn't all right. The situation was so dreadful it seemed unreal.

David's parents didn't move. The entire examination and brief words of mine had taken maybe ten minutes. Maybe less. They stood as they had when I entered the room, just as tense, just as stiff.

I walked with them toward the outside door. "I know how hard the next few hours will be for you. I'll meet you at the hospital in three hours, and we'll talk. We'll probably have some answers by then."

When I phoned the hospital I spoke to the brash young resident on the pediatric ward. "Jim, I'm sending you a two-and-a-half-year-old boy with signs of leukemia. Will you do a bone marrow and call the hematologist? I'll be down as soon as my clinic is over."

Jim, usually full of quips and questions about obscure diseases, didn't joke with me this time as he usually did. "Okay," he said simply.

o   o   o

I glanced out at the hills now darkened by the afternoon shadows. My next patient, Cathy, was a timid six-year-old recovering from pneumonia. Many years ago hearing "pneumonia" from a doctor must have brought the same terror into parents' hearts that hearing "leukemia" does today. Children used to die from pneumonia. Antibiotics hadn't been discovered. Nothing could be done to save them. Put us back in time half a century and I might be closing her eyes and turning away in sorrow from her dead body.

Cathy had picked the right time to be born and come down with pneumonia. I hadn't even put her in the hospital. She stayed at home in her own bed and took her antibiotics orally. In a week she was better. Now she sat smiling and holding out a few wilted flowers she had picked from her garden.

David. If it was leukemia, how long did David have to live? Had the bone marrow been done yet?

After Cathy, I saw two little adopted Vietnamese twins. They were lively as kittens. Neither the war, which separated them from their natural mother, nor near starvation, nor narrowly escaping death when the airplane they were on from Saigon crashed, had slowed them down. Between them they had IQs of at least three hundred, and two perforated eardrums. Nothing daunted them. Everyone in my office loved to see them. They were a reaffirmation of what children could go through and not be damaged.

The clinic ended. I glanced again at the hills. Months from now they would turn the color of old gold as the wild oats blossomed and went to seed. What condition would David be in then? I picked up my bag and headed for my car and the drive to the hospital. By now the bone marrow would have been done and the diagnosis would perhaps be definite.

                                      ❖   ❖   ❖

It's a short drive from my office to the hospital. Apricot orchards planted fifty years ago surround the hospital on three sides. Inside that large, modern, glass-and-concrete building seconds count as life begins and ends. Outside in the orchards the old trees move slowly through nature's cycle of dormancy, bloom and fruition.

I parked my car and walked toward the hospital entrance, pausing to look at the budding apricot trees. They'd been planted very precisely in neat rows. Their old trunks were gnarled and wrinkled. A brief rain had turned the bark black and shiny and raindrops still glistened on the branches. The tight pink buds and some already-opened flowers were bunched along the old wood, but rain had knocked many of the delicate buds to the ground. There they lay, pink drops against the wet soil. I shivered briefly and entered the hospital.

David's parents were sitting in the lounge. The concern on their faces made me suspend any extra words in my greeting. "Let me go check David's lab work," I said. "I'll be back in a few minutes."

I walked down the hall to the pediatric ward where David, worn out from the many strange rooms he'd been in that day, lay sleeping in a private room. An intravenous infusion was in his small arm. His hands were tied to the side of the crib to restrain them. His dark hair was wet from perspiration and tears. Bone-marrow tests can be both frightening and painful. He had kicked off his sheet, and I saw a large pink stain from Merthiolate over his hip. A small drop of fresh blood marked the spot where the bone-marrow needle had gone in. As I turned to pick up his hospital chart, the resident came into the room.

"It's leukemia," Jim said. "The bone marrow was filled with blasts. Lymphocytic type. He's certainly anemic. I've ordered a blood transfusion. I hate to see a child get that disease." He checked the IV infusion to see if it was running well. "Have you taken care of him for long?"

"I met him for the first time just three hours ago," I said. "His parents are in the lounge. I'd better go and give them the bad news."

Back in the lounge, Mr. and Mrs. Carver were still sitting in the same chairs. Mrs. Carver's hands were clasped so tightly in her lap that her fingers were white. Mr. Carver stood up and offered me his chair. I sat down and waited while he pulled up another one.

People know from a doctor's smile when good news is coming. But bad news? Terrible news? That's another matter. Where should I begin? I knew little about this family, not even if they had any other children. Both parents looked very young.

I put my hand over Mrs. Carver's. "David has leukemia," I said simply.

There, it was said! Whatever bargains they had tried to make with fate, whatever hopes they had hoped as they sat waiting for me were in that instant lost.

Mrs. Carver's hands were like ice. A mother, a father and a doctor who hadn't known each other several hours earlier were suddenly facing a bleak future. The bonds that carry us through terrible experiences are often formed at times of terrible prescience. Neither parent looked at me. I confess I was not trying to make eye contact with them.

"Let me tell you what I know about leukemia," I said. "First of all, it's usually fatal. It's a form of cancer of the white blood cells—*leuk* means 'white' and *emia* means 'blood.' What happens, for reasons no one yet knows, is that one type of white blood cell called a blast begins to grow in numbers. It crowds out the normal cells in the bone marrow that make blood. That's why David is anemic. The blast cell can't do a white blood cell's proper work either. White cells should protect the body from infection by latching onto bacteria and destroying them. But these abnormal cells take up space and do nothing. Consequently, a person with leukemia may die from an infection or from anemia. Now there are many things medicine can do. Blood transfusions can control the anemia. That's easy and fairly safe."

Mr. Carver shifted his legs awkwardly and leaned forward in his chair.

I continued. "There's another type of cell in the bone

marrow that gets crowded out—megakaryocytes. These make platelets—tiny particles that are needed for blood to clot. Without them we bleed to death. There are platelet transfusions available, and we can give them when David needs them.

"But it's infections that are so dangerous. Sometimes they can be controlled for a while with antibiotics. However, as time goes on, the infections become harder to treat, and eventually one will develop against which no antibiotic will work.

"David doesn't have any signs of infection now," I finished reassuringly. "He's going to feel much better when the transfusion is done. Then as soon as the hematologist sees him, we'll start treating the disease."

Tears ran down Mrs. Carver's cheeks and she wiped them away with the back of her hand. I sat back and took my hand from hers. "There are good, effective drugs with which leukemia can be treated, at least for a while," I said.

For the first time since I had sat down with them, she looked directly at me. Shock marred her young face. Her husband shifted uncomfortably in his chair. "How long— how long—" he began, and his voice faltered.

"How long will he live?" I filled in for him. He nodded. I pushed my chair back a bit. "If this were thirty years ago and we were sitting here, I would have said maybe six months or at best a year, because all we had then were blood transfusions and antibiotics. Then twenty years ago when steroids were used, I could have said maybe two years. But this is now, not then, and with our current therapy, children with leukemia do so much better than they used to. Three years, four years, even five years. And most important, these can be good years, years when they lead a very normal life.

"The treatment consists of a variety of oral drugs and

injections. Most of this can be given in the clinic. I'll put David in the hospital as little as possible—only if something comes up that can't be managed in the clinic. I'll be seeing you there every week, maybe several times a week."

It seemed to me the Carvers had relaxed a little. Mr. Carver took his wife's hand and held it.

"I've told you that leukemia is a fatal disease. Fifty years ago when children got tuberculosis or meningitis, they often died. There were no antibiotics and there was little a doctor could do. Sometimes a child did get well. Even with proven leukemia, years ago when there was no therapy, every once in a rare while a child would go into remission and be alive and seemingly healthy years and years later. Ostensibly those cases were cured, although we don't understand how.

"We don't know what causes leukemia; we don't have a cure. But new drugs are being tested all the time. I must caution you not to waste David's time and your money looking for miracles or phony cures. That's an expensive way to delude yourself and hurt David. We'll treat David's leukemia as if we may be able to cure it. Who knows what discoveries are just about to be published. I'll discuss all the therapy with you. I'll let you know all my ideas and where I get them and what we can expect from day to day, month to month and then, I hope, from year to year."

The Carvers looked at me blankly. If they could repeat a word that I had said, it would have surprised me.

"Let's go see David," I suggested. "He was asleep when I looked into his room."

We walked side by side down the long hospital corridor. The tall father put one foot in front of the other as if he were sleepwalking. The mother paced her steps to his. I walked slowly, a little behind them, thinking about other children I had cared for who had cancer.

Someone had written, "There's no way to justify the death of a child." Where had I read that? Here we were again, ready to try to outwit fate for a few precious years of a child's life. Was it better long ago when that struggle lasted only a few months?

I quickened my step to walk beside the Carvers. A nurse glanced at me and suspended her usual cheery greeting. She knew that my new patient had leukemia.

David was still sleeping. His sweat had dried, leaving tendrils of curls at his temples. His breath came in soft sighs. We watched him in silence. Anticipated loss is almost too poignant to bear. Who ever thinks about the true value of something when it's safely ours?

Each of us looked at this beautiful sleeping baby and no one spoke. It didn't seem possible that he might soon be dead. I could sense his parents' disbelief as they stared at him.

"He looks better already because of the transfusion," I said. "We'll start therapy and I'll see you here tomorrow." I left the room, relieved to be going home.

Outside the confines of the hospital the night was dark and pleasingly anonymous. Stars shone faintly over the shadowy orchards. I stood for a minute looking up at the stars and wished, like a child, that I would never, never be the parent in this sad situation.

That night as I tucked my children into their beds, I put my hand on their abdomens and surreptitiously felt to see if any one of them had an enlarged spleen. It would be months before I lost the need to reassure myself they didn't.

o   o   o

The next few days in the hospital proved no problem for David. Dr. Malick, our hematologist, wrote up a treatment plan to follow. We started David on Prednisone, a steroid hormone that works well with leukemia. It has the nice side effect of increasing the appetite and making the patient feel good.

We gave David intravenous injections of vincristine. Vincristine is made from alkaloid extracts of *Vinca rosea*, a cousin of the periwinkle plant, *Vinca minor*. Periwinkle is a common ground cover. Our hospital grounds are planted with it. This time of year it was in bloom with small, sky-blue flowers. If David had been older, I would have picked one and brought it to him and told him his medicine came from a flower. Someday I'll tell him, I promised myself.

Already I was thinking of a someday, of a future. David's death, foremost in my thoughts last night when I'd told his parents about leukemia, didn't seem quite so inevitable now that we had begun treatment.

Hope and future are so tightly linked. Had I given that small blue flower to young David he would probably have put it in his mouth. Would he one day be old enough to be charmed at the thought that a drug from a flower had saved his life?

Each morning when I met Mrs. Carver in David's room my news was good. David responded to the drugs beautifully. His bruises cleared. His enlarged spleen began to shrink to normal size. The leukemic cells disappeared from his bloodstream. It was hard to believe he had such a serious disease.

His mother and I watched him playing in his crib with a wooden puzzle, carefully putting the pieces in place. "He's pretty smart, isn't he?" I said.

"I don't have anything to compare him with," she answered modestly.

"Take it from an expert," I said with the greatest confidence I had shown since we met, "he's pretty smart," and she and I laughed together.

"What we're treating him with is the therapy decided on by cancer centers for children. It's the result of careful research. These centers tell us what drugs to use and what to expect in the way of bad reactions. We may have to modify the treatment, depending upon David's response."

Mrs. Carver reached into the crib and lifted her son. He clutched a puzzle piece in his fat little hand. He put it in his mouth and nestled against his mother's shoulder, watching me as we talked. Then with a little baby laugh he took the piece from his mouth and offered it to me. His mother and I laughed, too. Why shouldn't we? He was charming. He'd responded to the initial therapy better than I could have hoped.

And here we were. One week ago the Carvers had no idea what was in store for them. Now they had a child with a fatal disease. They'd have to develop a whole new frame of reference about life. No longer could they be secure about David's future and have pleasure planning for it. I had read that it is fortunate none of us know when our death will occur, for if we did, that knowledge would make our life unbearable. No matter when in the future our death might be, the thought of it would cross our minds so often that every day would be ruined. Who wouldn't try to find a way to evade the inevitable? The thought that we have control over our life is a shield few of us can put down. Health and dreams for the future are the very framework of that shield.

Our children are true extensions of ourselves. No adult when injured is ever as panic-stricken as a mother when her baby is hurt. A week or even an hour earlier she may have spanked the child or been irritated by it. But let its life be threatened and she knows absolute terror.

This young couple now could not escape the knowledge that the life span of their child was not only finite, but finite in well-defined statistical terms. How could one really deal with such a situation? I didn't know. The idea was overwhelming.

As days passed and David continued to do well, his parents relaxed and we spoke to each other with smiles in our voices.

The seventh morning of David's hospitalization, I asked them, "How would you like to take him home? He's responding beautifully. We're not doing anything for him here that can't be done in the clinic. You'll become familiar with all the drugs we use. He's only had two so far—the vincristine injections and the steroids. I want you to continue the steroid pills at home. I'll give him the vincristine injections once a week at the office. There are three other kinds of pills you'll have to give him, also."

Mrs. Carver counted on her fingers. "Now I see how nurses earn their money," she said with a laugh.

"The only reason I might have to readmit him to the hospital is if he develops an infection. That can be a problem. Antibiotics have to be started immediately if the infection is to be controlled, and since steroids may mask an infection, it's important that you call me anytime he doesn't feel well." This gloomy thought made me pause. I looked away from her to the floor but then recovered the hope in my voice.

"There's another way therapy has been improved just recently. Although it's new, I want David to have it—radiation to his brain. Children die from cerebral leukemia. The chemotherapy drugs we use don't get into two areas at all—the brain cells and the germinal cells in the testes. In the old days many children with leukemia under treatment would have no trace of the disease in their bloodstreams. Just when we thought they were cured, they'd develop severe headaches. We'd do a spinal tap and find leukemia cells in the spinal fluid. So we knew the leukemia cells were multiplying around their brains. This new treatment consists of irradiating the brain to kill any malignant cells there. The other spot, his testicles, we can check easily just by feeling them.

"I already did a spinal tap on David and injected methotrexate into his spinal fluid. That also decreases the chance of malignant cells growing around his brain. The spinal tap wasn't painful, but he had to be held tightly, which scares most children. Not David! He cried for a minute and then quieted down and just lay trustingly in the arms of the nurse. He's a wonderfully calm baby."

Mrs. Carver nodded her head and kissed David's cheek lightly.

"Here," I said, reaching into my bag and bringing out a sheaf of journal articles. "These are for you to read. The past few days I've reviewed the literature on leukemia. It's marvelously encouraging and speaks of fifty-percent cure rates with current therapy."

I handed Mr. Carver copies of the articles I had read. "A week ago I said that David's disease was fatal. I hadn't read up on leukemia then. My statement may already be out of date. I certainly hope it is.

"You can take David home. I'd like to see him at the clinic in two days. If anything worries you, telephone me. If there's anything you don't understand in the reprints, I'll translate the medical terms into plain English when I see you."

Mr. Carver took the reprints. They had titles like "Five-Year Survival Rates in Childhood Leukemia" and "Prevention of Central Nervous System Leukemia with Irradiation of the Brain." In them were years' of statistics gathered from cancer centers all over the country. Behind each statistic had once been two parents standing perhaps as were these parents, holding their baby, unsure and frightened about the future. The children in one series of statistics had died; died of infections, died vomiting blood, died in convulsions and in pain.

Then there was another column of figures. These children were still alive. Some were alive two years after diagnosis. Some were alive five years after diagnosis—and that was the criterion for cancer to be considered cured. Which column of statistics would this family fall into?

Safe in his mother's arms David regarded me with wide eyes. He's two and a half years old, I thought. In five years, if he lives, he'll be in second grade. Could that be possible? Would I be saying to these parents someday in the future, "David is cured."

I almost shook my head at my thought. It was really too much to expect. All my past medical experience spoke against it. But how marvelous that would be.

I wondered if Mrs. Carver had considered having another baby. At least then if David died she would still have a child to love. I decided to ask her when I knew her better.

I thought about David the next day but didn't hear from his parents. They must have things under control. The following morning they all arrived at the clinic. Wilma, my nurse, had been told to show them into an examining room immediately. I didn't want David sitting next to a child who had chicken pox. That might kill him if he caught it.

When I had told Wilma I had a new patient with leukemia whom we'd be treating in the clinic, she made an unpleasant face and said, "I hate that damn disease." Then she ordered the necessary drugs, needles and syringes.

"Call me when you're ready to give the injection," she said, "and I'll come and hold him still for you."

I opened the door to the examining room. The Carvers were standing in the same place they'd stood little more than a week ago. Gone was the tension present at our first meeting. Mr. Carver shook hands with me. The contact of our hands was firm and reassuring. Mrs. Carver smiled as if I were an old friend. She held David in her arms.

"He doesn't say many words yet but I've taught him your name. Come on, David," she coaxed, "you know it."

David looked shy and then, knowing how much it would please her, he flung his chubby arms up and said, "Docta Shark."

Mrs. Carver smiled with pride and sat her son on the examining-room table.

David looked like any healthy baby. His cheeks were pink, his fat little belly hung over the edge of his training pants. He didn't seem frightened at all.

So far so good, I thought. I wonder if he'll stay as calm when I approach him with a needle.

"How's everything going?" I asked. "How's his appetite?"

"He's turned into a little pig!"

Already David showed signs of the large doses of steroids we were using. He had become fatter and his face rounder.

David was playing with the blood-pressure cuff but didn't protest when I took it away from him. Instead he reached for the buttons on my white coat. I laid him down and felt for his spleen. It wasn't palpable. Wonderful! He had no enlarged lymph nodes, either. There were no new bruises on his skin, just a few fading spots where old ones had been. It was a perfectly normal examination. The prick on his finger where he'd had a blood test earlier wasn't oozing. I looked at the results of the test. There were no abnormal cells in his blood. He had a decreased number of white blood cells, and not many platelets either, but their level wasn't dangerously low. Not low enough to expect him to bleed into his brain. He didn't need another blood transfusion.

"David," I said, tying a tourniquet about his arm, "I'm going to put a needle in your arm. If you hold real still it won't hurt much, but if you wiggle around it will be very hard for me and I may have to stick you two or three times. I'll tell you when I'm ready and then you can yell, but keep your arm absolutely still.

"I want you to stay by him, Mrs. Carver. This should just take a minute. Wilma will steady his arm and I'm going to find a vein and inject the vincristine into it. It's apt to be difficult if he moves a lot."

How could someone David's age look at a needle and not pull away? I still shrink anytime I have to donate blood.

Only a most unusual two and a half year old would hold still for such a thing. David was that most unusual two and a half year old. When he'd been in the hospital, I'd let the resident draw all the blood and start all the IVs. I hadn't wanted my initial contact with David to consist of my hurting him. It's hard enough to get a small child not to be afraid of a doctor; sticking him with needles makes it almost impossible.

I wiped his skin with alcohol. Wilma held his arm firmly. His mother bent her head down to David's, keeping her face next to his.

"This is cold, David," I said, spraying ethyl chloride on his skin to numb it a little. "Be still now."

The needle went into a vein and blood filled the syringe. There hadn't been a murmur from David. I injected the medicine slowly. He didn't even flinch. Removing the needle, I held my finger over the prick to stop the bleeding. I was so pleased with his self-control. I put my arms around him to hug him and felt him stiffen. He suddenly looked as if he was going to cry. Imagine, he had enough trust in me to let me stick a needle in him, but not enough to let me hug him.

Mrs. Carver seemed relieved. She took David on her

lap. "Here are the prescriptions for the medicines you're to give him at home," I said. "The directions are on the bottles. The large white pill is cyclophosphamide. It may make his hair fall out, but fortunately that's only temporary. He must take the tiny six-mercaptopurine tablet every day, and the methotrexate pill once a week. I want to know immediately if he gets cramps or becomes constipated or develops sores in his mouth. Why don't you mash the pills in something sweet, like strawberry jam or chocolate syrup."

I didn't envy her the task of getting a child his age to swallow so many tablets.

"I've set up the appointments for his radiation therapy. It will take several weeks to complete. It won't hurt David, but again, being restrained is scary. I'll give you a sedative for him so he'll be groggy. It'll make it easier for him to lie still."

This was an appropriate time to ask, "Is there any possibility that you might be pregnant?"

"I guess I could be," she said. "I've missed two periods, but I just haven't had the time to see a doctor yet." She looked apprehensively across the room at her husband, whose eyes widened.

He came over to her, took David off her lap and, holding the child in one arm, put his other arm lovingly about her shoulders. They said good-by to me and were both smiling at each other as they walked out of my office.

The following week when David came in, he looked wonderful. Mrs. Carver said she was indeed pregnant and that her husband was delighted. He hadn't been as thrilled when they were expecting David, and she was a little surprised by this, but pleased.

It was obvious that David wasn't going to die suddenly. My confidence increased, and the Carvers' anxiety diminished.

David started radiation therapy. After the radiation to

his spine, the radiotherapist called me. He said he had been careful to irradiate the spine symmetrically so David's back wouldn't be crooked when he grew up. The experts were thinking sincerely in terms of *when* children with leukemia grew up, not *if* they grew up. I shared this good news with the Carvers.

I asked Mrs. Carver, "Did you have any problems getting him to take all those pills?"

"No, none at all," she said. "I mashed them up in apricot jam, then chocolate syrup. But what turned out to be best was mint ice cream. To encourage him, I eat a spoon of ice cream and then give him a spoonful with the pill hidden in it. I'd better stop or I'll get fat. Will I be glad when he finally learns how to swallow pills alone."

There we were—*when* was firmly part of our reality.

David, so small and yet already so much his own person, sat quietly on my examining table, listening. In the past weeks he'd been left in a strange bed in the hospital, had needles stuck into his spine and arms repeatedly and been immobilized for radiation therapy beneath a huge machine. Although I was sticking him with needles, he didn't shrink from me. He never fought back, never complained. Confident in his mother, he transferred this confidence to me. When I tickled his abdomen and made a game out of feeling for his spleen, he showed his trust by giggling playfully.

Wilma came into the examining room carrying the injection of vincristine.

If I stick him with a needle every time he sees me, I thought, soon there will be no smiling. How could I counteract that?

"Do you ever bribe him?" I asked his mother.

"It's never occurred to me to use a bribe. Even when I was toilet training him he just seemed to get the idea."

"I'm all for bribes," I said. "After all, these injections would be unpleasant for someone our age. Would you mind if I gave him a lollipop after each injection? As a reward for holding still."

"I'm sure he'd like that."

Wilma shook her head in mock disapproval and said, "You know lollipops will ruin his teeth." She took David's small arm and held it tightly so the needle would penetrate the vein cleanly and not leak the vincristine under his skin. That can make a painful sore.

David didn't smile at Wilma, but he held absolutely still. I found the vein, injected the medicine and withdrew the needle. That done, I reached into my pocket for a lollipop and handed it to him. He accepted it with the gravity of a king being paid tribute. It was his due. He didn't smile at me.

As the weeks passed, David seemed to thrive. His white count was low, but no cancer cells showed in the weekly blood counts. Each time the injections had to be given he held out his arm for Wilma to support. There was never a struggle or a howl, even though occasionally I had to stick him several times to find a vein. He accepted his lollipops as a just reward.

When the radiation therapy was completed, the radiotherapist sent me a letter which started, "Thank you for referring this lovely, easy to work with little boy." At less than three years of age, when other children were in the terrible twos, David impressed people as a lovely little boy.

His hair fell out, as we had known it would. One day he walked into my office quite bald. He wore a bright orange ski cap. It had a huge tassel and he put his hand to the tassel from time to time as if checking that it, too, hadn't fallen off. I removed the cap and ran my hand over his smooth head.

"What a beautifully shaped head he has. Are you sure he's not related to Yul Brynner?" I asked. Mrs. Carver laughed.

Everything had gone so unbelievably well the past few months that leukemia just didn't seem as dreadful a diagnosis as it had at first. The probability of David's death no longer blotted out our hopes for his future.

How I truly enjoyed this child! His mother loved him inordinately. I admired him just as inordinately. Look at the way he had taken all the therapy, including the radiation, without even a stomachache or one episode of vomiting. Clearly he was meant to be one of those children reported in the medical literature as cured.

After I had given him his injection I always reached into my pocket for the lollipop. The game was for him to guess what color it would be. He already knew all his colors.

o　o　o

As the months passed, David changed. His baby fat disappeared. His round face thinned out. His walk was more mature. He grew from a baby into a little boy. His speech developed rapidly. He now called me Dr. Sharkey without a trace of baby talk. Three years old is a turning point in a child's life. He moves out of babyhood.

Now when David came into the office, he would go directly to the examining-room table and climb onto it without any help.

Looking at Mrs. Carver I could see that David wasn't the only Carver who was growing. I was relieved that her pregnancy was going well. This new baby would be there for her if anything happened to David. But something happening to David seemed so remote I pushed it out of my mind.

o　o　o

One morning when they came to the clinic David felt warm. His temperature registered at 102 degrees. "Did he have a fever at home?" I asked.

"No," Mrs. Carver answered anxiously. "He's not acted sick at all. I would have called you if he had."

I examined David with extra care but could find no reason for the fever. He didn't look ill, but there was no disputing the thermometer. Perhaps the drugs that we gave him could account for the fever, but I doubted it. He must be developing an infection. What a thing to happen now when he had been doing so well. But that was a common story with this terrible disease. The leukemia inactive, no trace of abnormal cells anywhere in his body, a child would suddenly develop a fever and be dead from infection in an unbelievably short time.

My concern showed in my voice. "I'm going to put him in the hospital. I can't find the reason for this fever. It's not very high, but it worries me just the same. I'll treat him with huge doses of antibiotics and if the fever's due to infection, that may check it. The fever may be caused by some virus, but that can be dangerous, too. Take him to the hospital now. I'll call the resident. He'll start the antibiotics and I'll be down in a while."

Mrs. Carver didn't say anything to me. Her face showed her fear.

"Are you all right?" I asked. "Can you drive there safely?"

"Yes," she answered.

Once again they left the office. Her husband wasn't here to help this time.

I should have known David's course had been too good to be true, I thought bitterly as I telephoned the resident.

At lunchtime I drove to the hospital. The flowers on the apricot trees had given way to fuzzy little balls of new fruit. I took the elevator to the pediatric ward. David had been put into a crib, and there he sat playing with another wooden puzzle with his one free hand. His other arm was immobilized by the intravenous line.

Strange as it seems, the exact reason a person's temperature rises with an infection is unknown. Many things can cause a fever, but bacteria in the bloodstream is the dreaded one when a child has leukemia. A culture of David's blood had already been drawn. Perhaps it would grow bacteria. Then and only then would I know exactly what infection David had and be able to treat it specifically. But it takes at least twelve hours and sometimes several days for a blood culture to turn positive. David could be dead by then. In the interim I'd give him huge doses of three different antibiotics and hope one of them would work.

Despite his fever David didn't look especially ill. Mrs. Carver stood anxiously by the side of his bed. Her hand grasped the side rail of the crib as if she needed it for support. She turned toward me when I entered the room, her eyes dark. She said she hadn't been able to reach her husband by phone. I'd never seen such fear on her face. It was even worse than when David had been hospitalized the first time.

I went straight to her and put my arm about her. I thought she might actually faint. "He looks good," I said reassuringly. "I'm not even sure he has an infection yet. It's just that we can't wait. We've got to stay ahead of the germs."

She shook her head, shuddered and blinked back sudden tears.

"I know you're scared," I said. "I was too when I read that thermometer. But just look at him. This is probably a false alarm." She was breathing rapidly, maybe from fear or perhaps because her pregnancy was so advanced. "When is the baby due?" I asked, concerned that this shock might make her go into labor prematurely.

"In a month."

"Have you been feeling all right?"

"I haven't even thought about it much. But I wanted to

ask you—I want you to tell me honestly—about the new baby—what chance—" Her words stopped. She looked away from me.

"What are the chances of the new baby having leukemia?" I suggested. She nodded and more tears ran down her face. "Just about the same as being struck twice by lightning," I said, thinking unhappily that lightning does strike more often in the same place. Still it seemed like an appropriate thing to say. "Don't give it a second thought. Do you want a boy or girl?" I tried to distract her.

Her voice trembled as she answered, "I just want a healthy baby."

In his crib David played, not noticing his mother's tears. "Have you told him about the new baby yet?"

"Yes, we got a little book with pictures, but he didn't seem interested. I let him feel the baby kick once and now he's always asking if it's wiggling."

David, I prayed fervently, get over this infection. Don't die now, just before the baby comes. Wait until your mother is stronger and the baby's doing well. Wait until we're all more prepared for your death. Please, get better this time.

My heart ached as I looked at this beautiful child playing in his crib, as unaware of what fate held in store for him as of the place he held in his mother's heart and in my heart, too.

We had all been so reassured by his benign course. Now I realized how foolish we were. Even if he did well this time, there would be a next time—or a next. And it was never going to be any easier.

Whether it was prompt antibiotic therapy that stopped an infection or if I'd treated a fever due to a cold, I never knew. The blood cultures remained sterile. Despite the high fever, which lasted for three days, David never seemed very ill. Each day when I came to see him, he smiled and reached out to me. He was happier than most children in the hospital. His mother, of course, was always with him.

One evening I stopped by the hospital to check on him and met his paternal grandparents. The grandfather's briefcase lay on the floor by David's crib. He must have just come from his office. The grandmother was a beautiful woman with a charming Scottish accent. She moved toward me the minute I entered the room, warmly taking my hands in hers.

"I've heard so much about you," she said. "My daughter-in-law Betty always talks about you. We all feel we know you. I'm so glad to finally meet you. I used to be a nurse. I even took care of a child with leukemia years ago. Betty showed me the medical articles you gave her. I read them over and over. Everything was so mysterious in my day. Our doctors never gave out medical articles. What you're doing is so much better. We feel like we're all important to David's care, too."

We watched David for a few minutes and then stepped outside the room. The grandmother's vivacity left her as she asked hesitantly, "Is he going to be all right—this time?"

"It certainly looks like it," I said. "I thought he'd be a lot sicker than he was with this fever, and I'll admit I was worried. You and I know how quickly a baby with leukemia can go downhill. Was it about twenty years ago when you were nursing your patient with leukemia?"

She nodded her head in agreement.

"You'll notice in those reprints they use the word 'cured.' That's something quite new. I never thought in my lifetime I'd hear the term 'cured' applied to leukemia."

"Neither did I," she said. "I can hardly believe it."

"I'm absolutely amazed at how well David's done. He's really a remarkable child. Made of good stuff." I smiled.

"Strong Scottish genes on my side of his family," said

his grandmother. "But do you know what Betty's family is?"

"No," I said. "I wondered if she was Italian."

"She's a Navajo Indian."

"I might have guessed," I laughed. "That explains why David never flinches when I stick him."

After five days of antibiotic treatment I sent David home from the hospital, as well as if nothing had happened. What a marvelous little boy. He had weathered this fever well. Hope crept in again. My confidence returned again.

David's grandmother brought him in for his next appointment. "Betty's so tired," she said. "The baby's due any day. I'm going to keep David at my house when she goes to the hospital." David climbed onto the examining-room table. Without his mother here would he be as brave as usual?

"Do you want your grandma or Wilma to hold your arm this time?" I asked.

David looked slowly from Wilma to his grandmother, as if to play favorites. They both smiled at him.

"No one," he said in a firm voice that sounded delightfully grown-up.

"All right, David," I said. "But if you move your arm even a little bit the needle will slip and I'll have to stick you again. Are you sure you don't want someone to hold your arm?"

"No," he said again.

Skeptically I took his arm and without any trouble stuck the needle right into a vein. He didn't move an inch. Wilma, who had held countless screaming, thrashing children for injections, was amazed.

"I've never seen a child hold still like that for a needle," she said. "Never. How old did you say he was?"

"Three, going on thirty," I said with a laugh.

*   *   *

The next time his grandmother brought David to the clinic she had with her a fidgety five-year-old girl for whom she occasionally baby-sat. The child was the complete opposite of David. She nervously walked all about my office, picking up instruments and opening cabinet drawers. I sat her down in a chair with a picture book, but she didn't stay put for long. She simply would not be still. Because of her, David's grandmother and I couldn't talk comfortably. I examined David quickly and gave him the vincristine injection while the girl climbed up on a chair and tried to take a picture off the wall.

"She's hyperactive," said his grandmother apologetically. "Her pediatrician put her on Ritalin recently, but I can't see that it's done any good. She's always into something. She's just—well, she's just nothing like David. I sometimes think it's so unfair—" Her eyes went from David sitting calmly on the table to the girl now lying on the floor.

I nodded. We looked away from each other, embarrassed by our thoughts. The girl suddenly jumped up from the floor and gave David's leg a sharp jerk, almost pulling him off the table. She giggled.

"It would be wise to keep them apart," I said. "David doesn't need any broken bones."

"I know what you mean," said the grandmother.

*   *   *

When her time came, Mrs. Carver went to the hospital and gave birth to a healthy boy. I examined him when he was two hours old and took him from the nursery to his mother. I put him in her arms.

"Look," I said. "He's completely normal and the image of his brother."

"I was so worried," she said. "Is everything really all right?"

"Absolutely perfect."

"We're going to call him John."

As I gathered up the baby in my arms to return him to the nursery, she reached out and touched my arm. "I'd like it if you'd call me Betty and my husband Stan from now on."

"Betty," I said, "you and Stan have the most beautiful baby in the nursery."

In the nursery I put John back in his bassinet and looked closely at his face. He really was a tiny duplicate of David. My heart sank. Now something surely would go wrong with David.

o   o   o

David became very much the big brother. He thought it strange that John had appointments with me, too. After all, I was *his* doctor. When Betty brought John to my office for his first well-baby check, David carried a baby doll as large as his little brother. He put the doll proudly on the examining table next to John and told me, "Momma has a baby. I have a baby, too."

"There's no male chauvinism there," I laughed. "You're really raising him well, aren't you, Betty?"

David watched as I injected the new baby against diphtheria, tetanus and whooping cough. Years ago any one of these diseases might have been fatal. Someday in the future we would probably have a vaccine against leukemia as well.

o   o   o

Summer passed to autumn. Fallen apricots lay on the dry earth under the orchard trees. Winter came and golden leaves carpeted the ground. The trees and the mountains stood bare. At last the rains started. Green mountains again filled the view from my office window.

David, now three and a half, was as smart as any five year old. I looked forward to his visits, not only because he was doing so well but because he was so much fun to talk with. Although he had a large vocabulary he never said anything that wasn't pertinent. He was wonderfully intelligent.

One day he came into my office so angry he could hardly look at me. I put my arms around him but he pulled back and two tears welled up in his eyes.

"David," I said, reaching for his hands, "what's wrong?"

His voice trembled. "I thought you were *my* doctor."

David turned his head and refused to look at me. I was puzzled.

"Of course I am. What makes you think I'm not?"

Betty solved the mystery. "A little girl in the waiting room just said that you were *her* doctor and David insisted you were *his*. They almost came to blows over you."

I picked David up and held him close. "I am your doctor, David. I may see other children but I will always be your doctor."

His anger disappeared. Now he let me hug him.

As they were leaving, Betty asked me, "Do you think I should let him go to nursery school? All the children his age on our street are going."

He'd love it, I thought, but what if he caught chicken pox? "No, it's taking too much of a chance," I said. "I don't want him exposed to any contagious diseases. He'll start kindergarten in two years and we'll have to worry about that then. Let's play it safe."

Kindergarten in two years!

∘ ∘ ∘

John grew also. Although he looked like David, he had a very different temperament. He cried and cried when I gave him an injection and he didn't forgive me, either. Months later when he came back to my office, he'd begin to cry as soon as he caught sight of me.

One Halloween David came into the office dressed as Jesse James. A cowboy hat sat on his black Indian hair. He had double guns slung around his waist and a huge grin on his face.

"What's this?" I exclaimed. "The most handsome cowboy in the West? Please don't shoot me. Give me a hug instead," which he did. "But shouldn't you be an Indian chief?"

"I'm a cowboy," David insisted.

Betty smiled. "My father must be turning over in his grave, but that's what David wants, so that's what he is."

David nodded. "Next year I'll be an Indian."

How different my thoughts were from those I'd had when David first came into my office. He was sturdy and happy. All the medicines he took and the weekly blood tests had become a comfortable routine. We had again lost our fear of the disease. It seemed natural to think he would someday go to college.

Because of the medicines, David had an abnormally low white blood cell count. Even so, he had fewer colds than many children in my practice. Once he developed a middle-ear infection. I was very concerned when I saw that red eardrum. How should I treat it? One antibiotic would do for a normal child. Should I put David in the hospital again and use huge doses of antibiotics? There was no positive answer. I decided to use two antibiotics and keep him at home. I worried for a week until it became obvious the ear infection was healing nicely. Highly relieved, I gained confidence that David could manage infections despite his low white count.

* * *

Betty became pregnant again, and this time the Scottish genes finally had their chance to show. The new baby, Mary, was fair and blond. John was fiercely jealous of her. He clung to his mother all day and cried. Betty didn't dare leave the new baby unattended for a minute. Once John had pulled her out of her crib. Betty was afraid he might inadvertently hurt Mary.

David greeted Mary's arrival with the same equanimity with which he had welcomed John's. He even tried to change her diapers but was so afraid of sticking her with the diaper pins that he never could get the diaper together.

However, what impressed David far more than his new sister was his new bicycle. His father insisted on buying one. I tried my best to talk him out of it. All the boys in the neighborhood had bicycles, he said. "But what if David falls off?" I asked.

Stan's face said more clearly than words, "Sissy woman doctor." Then he looked uneasy. Was there something I was keeping from him?

"No," I said, "bicycles worry me. We always have at least one child in the hospital with a broken leg or fractured skull from falling off a bike. I'd be saying the same thing if— if David didn't have—leukemia." I stumbled on the word.

We sat in awkward silence. "Oh, all right," I said finally, "get him a bike. He can't be different from all the other children in the neighborhood. But please, leave the training wheels on—always."

School time was approaching. David was five years old and excited about going to kindergarten. He still took all the pills, but without the ice cream—just swallowed them down. Supervising the medicines was as routine for his mother as making breakfast.

One September afternoon David appeared in my office carrying a shiny lunch box. "I went to school today," he said proudly. How was it possible these three years had passed so quickly?

"What should I tell his teacher?" Betty asked.

"I'll write her a letter. Nothing special is needed. If he has a fever he should be sent home at once. And as for climbing on the monkey bars—" I hesitated. I felt the same about monkey bars as I did about bicycles. "God forbid he falls, but I expect we'll harm him more if we try to restrict what he does than if we let him take his chances. When it comes to things like climbing, there's no way you can limit children except by tying them up!"

"I don't fall," said David. "I can climb like Spider-man."

"David's really careful," said Betty. "He's never been hurt. Fortunately he doesn't dare things."

"And, oh yes," I reminded her, "if anyone in school has chicken pox, keep David home. For that matter if any illness is going around, keep him home."

Once again I thought, if we discontinued the anti-cancer therapy we could stop worrying about infections. But then suppose his leukemia came back? There were no answers.

David took to school the same way he did to everything else—with perfect confidence. His teacher loved him. The calm, intelligent, sweet kind of child he was brings out the best in everyone.

His teacher phoned me several times. She wanted to know all about leukemia. She wanted to know if he should be treated like the other children. Should he be given the same amount of work? Should he be allowed to play in the schoolyard? Did he need an extra rest period? My answer was to treat him as a normal, healthy child.

I said to her, "Don't tell the other children he has leukemia. They might not want to play with him and it could scare some ignorant parents who think it's contagious. We don't want David to seem different; that's hard for any child. Just think if the other children taunted him that he was going to die."

I heard the teacher sigh on the other end of the telephone. "I know, they do say things like that."

"David's been treated for three years," I told her. "There's no evidence that the disease is even present anymore. I don't want to have cured him only to have him grow up with the idea that there's something wrong with him. So just treat him as you do the rest of the children."

Since it would be a shame for him to miss school, I cut his office visits to every other week. The first few times that I didn't see him weekly, I telephoned his mother to check if all was well. After a while I stopped. Nothing was going to happen. Two weeks could go by now without my giving a single thought to David.

o   o   o

In the past three years several new drugs had been released for the treatment of leukemia.

"They're good backup drugs if we need them," Dr. Malick said. "At least we'll have something to treat him with if he relapses."

"That's a pretty big *if,* isn't it?" I asked. "He's gone for three years with no problems. Don't you suppose he's one of the children who is cured?"

"I never use that word," Malick said reprovingly. "In spite of what the literature says, someone can relapse years and years after you think he's cured."

Then I asked something I had thought about frequently. "How long shall we keep him on therapy?"

"I honestly don't have the answer," Malick said. "Most of the children in the literature were treated for two or three years, but everything is going so well with David we certainly don't want to change anything we're doing right now."

o   o   o

The kindergarten year passed quickly without incident. So did first grade. David learned to read and to swim. Stan had taken the training wheels off the bicycle long ago. David was one of the tallest boys in his class. He was delighted to be so big and strong. Now when he came into the office he would pull off his shirt with a flourish and flex his biceps for me.

"What big muscles you have," I'd say admiringly.

"Do you want to feel them?" he'd offer with pride.

For the past five years I had examined him every week or two. I knew every part of his body better than my own children's. My routine was so well known to us that I could do it automatically. Look in his ears, listen to his chest, feel for any nodes, palpate over his spleen and then at the end carefully feel the size and shape of his testes. When he was a baby this part of the exam was like any other part. But now he became aware that I was violating his privacy. As I pulled down his underpants, he reached for them and pulled them right back up. He held them tightly to him and giggled when I tried to remove them again. His mother and I exchanged amused glances. David was certainly growing up.

Although I didn't expect the disease to recur after all

these years, I nevertheless always examined David's testes. Now what could I do about his new-found modesty?

"Young man," I said, "if what I do makes you giggle," and I reached again for his underpants as he clutched them closer to him, "well, then you'll just have to giggle. But I have to examine all of you."

Nonplussed, he loosened his grip on his underpants. I was so familiar with the size and shape of his little testes that I didn't have to look at them while I felt them. If they had changed the slightest bit, my fingers would have recognized it.

Of all the parts of David's body that I checked so frequently, his testes were very important. If his leukemia were to become active again that was the first place it might show up. His brain we had cleared of malignant cells by irradiation. There was no recommendation that the testes be irradiated or removed surgically to prevent a relapse of the disease.

But there was no deviation to worry me. All the changes in David's body were normal. He was taller. Muscles had replaced his baby fat. He lost his front baby teeth and permanent teeth had filled the spaces.

His vocabulary also grew and was wonderfully descriptive. He always had a story to tell me about something that had happened to him, a circus where a bear had almost stepped on him, a wave that had knocked him down at the beach, a race he had won at school. His enthusiasm was delightful.

On a Monday afternoon Dr. Malick telephoned me and said, "I've just come back from a conference on leukemia. It's time to stop David's therapy."

He took me by surprise. I said uneasily, "Why do you think it's time?"

"I discussed his case at the conference," he said. "We

went over survival rates in all the studies, and there's no difference between the children who were treated for two years or for three years. David's already exceeded the time most children have been treated. Everyone recommended that we stop therapy."

I was alarmed at the thought. "What will happen if we take him off the drugs and he relapses?"

"According to the statistics, if a child is going to relapse he will even if he's still on therapy," Malick said. "We can't keep him on the drugs forever."

I didn't want to give this news to Betty over the telephone. David had an appointment with me in two more days. When they came into the office, David started to climb onto the table as usual.

"Wait a minute," I said. "Don't climb up there today. Today is special. I've something to tell you that makes it so." David paused and smiled at me but climbed onto the table anyway. Betty looked puzzled.

"Dr. Malick presented David's case to a conference at the medical school. They recommended that we stop all therapy. He's been treated several years longer than some of the children they consider cured. I never thought that in my lifetime I would be talking about cures when it came to leukemia, but here we are. I can hardly believe I'm saying this, but today we stop his drugs."

David didn't look impressed. His mother had moved to one side of him, and I stood on his other.

"What shall I do with all the pills I have left?" Betty asked.

That question was not as simple as it seemed. "Do you really think he's cured?" was the message I got. I know I wanted to believe he was. Hadn't his course followed the exact course of the cases reported as cured?

How could I answer her? I could only tell her what I

would have wanted to hear had I been asking the question about my own son.

"Don't put the medicines on the shelf," I said. "Throw them away. If we ever need them again, we'll cross that bridge when we come to it. Let's have faith in what we read and in how well David has done. I still want to see him every week and check his blood count until we're confident that the disease is truly gone. Then I'll see him less and less frequently."

"David," I said, taking his hands in mine, "we're going to stop your medicines. You don't have to take pills anymore. I'll bet you can't even remember when you didn't have to swallow all those pills, can you?"

David shook his head.

"Do you remember what the pills were for?"

Again he shook his head.

I had told him when he started kindergarten that he had to take the pills and have injections because he had some bad white blood cells. I'd drawn him a picture of a white blood cell that looked like a face with a frown. The pills would keep this bad cell away. The disease he had, I told him, was called leukemia and he'd already had it for three years. It could be a bad disease and make him die, but he was doing just fine, I quickly reassured him. I had asked him at the time, "Do you know what most little boys die from?"

David had shaken his head. "Cars," I had said, "automobile accidents. But you won't die that way because you keep your seat belt on, and you don't have to worry about the leukemia because you take your pills."

That seemed to make sense to him. I had mentioned death because I was afraid David might overhear a conversation about leukemia or have some child at school taunt him that he was doing to die. I didn't think any more explanation was necessary. There wasn't a fearful bone in this child's body. He had faith in his parents, my word and himself. I didn't want that shaken.

"Do you remember those bad white cells I once told you about a long time ago?" I asked him. "They're all gone. They've been gone for such a long time that I don't think they'll come back. We'll still have to do blood tests, but you don't have to have any more pills or injections."

"Will I still get a lollipop?" he asked.

"Of course," I said, hugging him. "And today you may have a whole handful." I patted his bottom. "Out you go, back to school."

David skipped out of the room, lollipops filling each hand. Betty and I followed him into the hall. Neither she nor I knew quite what to do. We stood awkwardly while David pulled the cellophane off one of the lollipops. For five years I had followed a protocol. Now the security of that routine was gone.

Betty and I looked at each other. She reached out her arms to me at the exact moment I held mine out to her. There in the clinic hall we embraced. I saw, over her back, David's embarrassed expression and Wilma's startled face. Betty started to cry, and my eyes filled with tears. I turned, my arm about her, and led her back into the privacy of the examining room. Words were unnecessary. The tears ran down our faces as we smiled and smiled at each other. Finally I found some tissues and said, "What a couple of silly geese we are. We're embarrassing David." We dried our tears and left the room in as dignified a fashion as we could.

Wilma waited discreetly until the outside door closed behind David and Betty. "What's happened?" she asked urgently.

"Wilma," I said, "I just told Betty to stop David's medicines. I told her he was cured."

"Good heavens!" Wilma said. "When I saw you both crying I was sure David had relapsed. Cured! Can you imagine that!" She walked away shaking her head and smiling.

Our confidence in David's health seemed borne out by time. I examined him and tested his blood every week. Everything remained normal. I dropped his visits to every other week and then to every third week. Sometimes I would call Betty just to hear that he was in school and all was well.

"I miss him," I said.

"I miss you," she answered. "Seeing you every week was sort of like seeing my mother."

Did I dare stretch his visits to once a month? I decided to do so one day when David would have had to miss a school party to keep his appointment.

"If he has bruises, swollen glands or fever, call me," I told Betty. "Otherwise bring him in the first of every month."

A month was such a long time. I watched David leave my office with the apprehension of a mother watching her child go off to kindergarten. I didn't really want to let go, but I knew he would benefit psychologically from fewer medical visits. I also knew I could check his blood count every day and not pick up a relapse one day sooner than it would manifest itself by a swollen gland or a large bruise. In the process of following him so closely for his physical health, I could end up with a youngster who was emotionally destroyed by anxiety.

o   o   o

Now that I only saw David monthly, I was always startled at how much he grew in so short a time. His conversations became more adult. He had stories about his best friend and stories about a stray kitten he had brought home that his mother had let him keep. He talked excitedly about places he wanted to go—Disneyland and Hawaii. He never brought up his leukemia.

My office walls were filled with pictures he had drawn at school for me. He had won the battle for long hair with Betty, and his thick black hair now reached well below his ears. He could have easily passed for an Indian child from a century ago. His mother and I were more enamored of him than ever. He accepted this with natural grace.

To my horror one day David, John and Mary came into the office covered with chicken pox. Thank God we had taken him off the therapy, I thought. This previously dreaded disease proved to be no problem for him. One pox he scratched left a scar on his cheek.

"If Mary had scratched there it really would be too bad," I told Betty. "But David's beard will cover the scar someday."

o   o   o

The year David had his eighth birthday I decided to spend my summer vacation as a volunteer doctor for a hospital in India.

"I'll be away for two months," I told Betty. "Dr. Malick will take care of David while I'm gone. But there's still a lot of time before I'll be leaving."

As I talked to her, I ran my hands over David's familiar body. He was, despite the radiation therapy and drugs, a big child. Recently his body shape had matured and his muscles were chunkier. As usual, at the end of the exam I felt his testes. David no longer giggled the way he had when he was younger but tolerated this patiently. All at once I was alarmed. Was I imagining it or did his testes feel larger? There were no hard lumps and there was nothing irregular about them, but they definitely had increased in size.

"David," I said, "let me have a look. I think you're growing up a bit."

I felt both testes again. I was worried. If they had not been David's I would have thought them normal. Against there being any malignancy present was the fact that both testes felt the same, and at eight years old there may be a slight increase in testicular size.

Betty's face lost its color as she watched me. I turned to her and tried to keep anxiety out of my voice. "Both his testes are a tiny bit larger. But they are soft and smooth. I think it's because he's maturing a bit. Still, I want to check them every week for a while."

Reassuring as I tried to sound to her, I was not reassured. That week I examined the testes on every eight-year-old boy who came into my office. What Phillip, who had a cold, or Tom, who came in to have his eyes checked, thought about having his pants pulled down, I couldn't even consider. I had to examine enough boys that age to convince myself that David's testes were really normal. And they seemed to be. Week after week I carefully measured and felt his testes, and week after week they remained the same size. I spoke to Malick about this.

"Just keep doing what you're doing," he said. "If the testes continue to grow larger, they should be biopsied and then irradiated."

I was terribly upset at the thought that leukemia cells might be in his testes right now, just waiting to spread to other parts of his body and kill him. "Why don't we irradiate his testes anyway? I was going to discuss vasectomy with David when he grows up because with all this therapy he'd have a right to worry about producing an abnormal baby."

"No," said Malick. "Irradiating the testes will leave him sterile. It's not recommended therapy."

Weeks went by and David's testes didn't get any larger. His blood count remained normal. Perhaps I was too anxious, I thought. I decided to see him only every other week.

o   o   o

My vacation time arrived. "I hate to go away now," I told Malick, "but I've committed myself to work in that hospital in India. Anyway, I suspect my patients' mothers are beginning to think me strange because every eight-year-old who comes in gets his testes examined."

Malick laughed. "You're too involved with David. A little distance will be good for you, although India is a bit excessive. I'll take good care of him. Don't worry."

It was easy to put my practice in order. I gave my problem patients to other doctors for the time I would be gone. Some I would wonder about while I was away. The little boy recovering from a severe head injury received when he was hit by a car was just starting to improve and know where he was. The next months would be critical for him. Then there was a premature baby who couldn't breathe without the help of a respirator. She was so fragile and tiny that anything might happen to her in two months. And Theresa, a teenage girl badly crippled with rheumatoid arthritis—I'd had her in the hospital for half of the year. She was so depressed she wouldn't even get out of bed. A fine psychiatrist had been seeing her daily, and Theresa had just begun to take a little interest in life. I'd write to her often from India to let her know I cared.

Who else was there I'd worry about? David? No. The episode with his testes had been nothing but a bad scare. He'd be in good hands. I'd send him postcards just because I loved him.

o   o   o

I found India depressing. Drugs were in short supply. Equipment was scarce. I improvised as best I could. Most of the children's illnesses were complicated by malnutrition. Some children rallied and lived. Many died. Whether they got well or died, their beds were quickly filled by others just as desperately ill.

At the airport, before boarding the plane for the United States, I sent another postcard to David.

o　o　o

It was fall in the valley when I arrived home. The mountains were brown. My first day back at the office was so busy I only glanced at them once.

Wilma told me all my patients had done well while I was away. The child who had been injured in the automobile accident had been discharged from the hospital and was recovering nicely. I telephoned his parents. They had an appointment to bring him to my office next week. I also called David, but no one answered the phone at his home.

A real delight was waiting for me at the hospital. The little premie who had been on a respirator when I left was now a lovely baby, breathing normally.

Theresa's rheumatoid arthritis was better, and she was beginning to develop that heroic strength of character that children who live with a chronic disease must have. I sat on the edge of her bed and we talked for a while. Then I went out to the doctors' desk where the charts were kept to catch up on her course over the past two months. As I sat there, an intern and a resident came by making their evening rounds. They were discussing each patient briefly.

"Welcome back," one said. "You've got Theresa's chart. She did really well while you were gone. She even gets up and walks to physical therapy now."

Leaving me, they went on to talk about the next patient. Although I was reading Theresa's chart I could hear their words.

"In this room is a child with leukemia in relapse—"

Suddenly Theresa's chart felt as if it weighed a hundred pounds. Unconsciously I held my breath, waiting for their next words.

"Whose patient is it?" the resident asked the intern.

"Dr. Malick's."

Thank God! Not David, I thought with relief. But then a terrible thought occurred to me. Malick had many patients with leukemia, and I had left David in his care.

I put down Theresa's chart. I had to find out who that child was. The name would be on a chart. I started at the top of the chart rack. Slowly I read the name of every patient. There on a chart was what I dreaded, "David Carver–Dr. Malick."

I picked it up and opened it. What had happened? How long ago? What was being done? I felt sick as I skimmed through the doctor's notes.

In Dr. Malick's hard-to-interpret scrawl, I read that David had been fine for six weeks after I left for India. Malick had seen him at two-week intervals. Only a few days before my return one of David's testes had developed a small hard spot. He had been admitted for a biopsy. His blood count was normal. In the hospital Malick repeated David's bone-marrow test. We'd done this periodically over the past six years in the clinic. It had always been normal. This time the bone marrow showed malignant cells. This meant the leukemia had already spread from the testes. There was no point to doing a biopsy now. Both of David's testes were to be irradiated tomorrow, and he was to start a new course of chemotherapy. My heart ached as I put the chart back in the rack and walked into David's room.

David was sitting in bed watching television. He was as beautiful as when I had last seen him, and he looked just as healthy. His cheeks were rosy. His hair was shorter and it made him look more grown-up. His face lit up when he saw me and he held out his arms. I hugged him and, keeping him in my arms, sat on the edge of his bed. I had no idea what he'd been told.

"David," I said, "yesterday I was in India, with elephants and palaces, but I can't tell you how glad I am to be back. I didn't know you were in the hospital. Tell me what's been happening."

Shyly David said, "Oh—I—well—"

"Did the leukemia come back?" I asked.

He nodded his head. "Down there," he said, pointing. "I'm going to have X-rays tomorrow."

"Are you scared?"

He didn't answer for a minute. Then he nodded his head.

"Don't be," I said. "X-rays don't hurt. When you were a baby we gave you X-rays to your head. I'm sure you don't remember, but I do. The X-rays will kill all the bad cells. Does anything hurt now?"

"No."

"May I take a look?" I ran my hands over his neck. No enlarged nodes. Over his abdomen. No palpable spleen. His liver felt normal. Pulling down his pajamas, I looked at his testes. Carefully I put my finger on the left one. It had a hard lump in it. This was what I had been fearful of finding for so many years, I thought bitterly.

I gave David a gentle hug and left the room. Once away from him anger came over me. We had irradiated his brain at the time of diagnosis to prevent a relapse. Why were the testes considered so sacred?

My next thought upset me greatly. Would the recommendations in a few years be to irradiate the testes also, as part of the initial therapy? David would then be one of the statistics that might get formulated into future cancer therapy. But it was too late for David already.

The next day his testes were irradiated. The lump disappeared but otherwise they still looked normal. Hope again distorted reality. When David grew up I'd give him testosterone, I decided, so he'd mature sexually and he wouldn't need to consider a vasectomy.

Of course, my "when" was no longer as definite as it had been earlier. I told myself that since the source of David's relapse had been removed and the disease was being treated with a new chemotherapeutic drug, this would work, just as previous therapy had.

I read the most recent medical literature on leukemia. What I learned depressed me. When leukemia recurred only in the testes, there was still a fairly decent cure rate. When the leukemia recurred in only the bone marrow, there was also a sizable cure rate. But if at the time of relapse, malignant cells were discovered in both the testes and the bone marrow, the chance of a child living more than a year was slight.

Still, some children did live. Please, I prayed, let David be one of them.

After David went home from the hospital I continued his therapy in the clinic. The new drugs gave him such terrible abdominal cramps he couldn't go to school.

The next two weeks dragged by slowly. The drugs depressed his white count, but that had happened before and not hurt him. His appetite was poor. His face lost its roundness and his cheekbones became prominent. In only a few weeks he looked years older.

I had again shown the new medical literature to his mother and father. We had not said much to each other since the relapse. We waited to see if the new treatment would work. We'd had our miracle and although it had proven false once, none of us was willing to give up our hopes that David would respond to therapy again.

After a month it was time for another bone-marrow

test. This one, too, was full of malignant cells. Dr. Malick came up with another new drug to add to David's therapy.

°   °   °

As often happens when you're preoccupied with a medical problem, you come across frequent references to it in medical journals, in colleagues' talk, even in the newspapers. Never before had I seen so many articles on leukemia.

Every year our hospital sponsors a conference on an important aspect of medical care. In past years subjects had been the premature infant, the treatment of shock, and advances in antibiotic therapy. This year the conference was to be on childhood cancer. Leading experts, the men who wrote the papers I read and formulated the therapy with which we treated David, would be the speakers. Dr. Malick and I drove to the conference together.

"We'll have the chance to get the latest information now," he told me as we sped down the highway in his little sports car. "Maybe there's some new therapy that hasn't been published yet that we can give David if he doesn't respond."

The conference lasted a full day. All the speakers had many slides. They showed comparisons of different drugs and their toxicities and graphs with the children's survival in years. However, the real message was in the pictures of the affected children.

"This is Patty, age two at the time of diagnosis of acute lymphocytic leukemia," said one speaker. Projected on the large screen was a pale and miserable-looking baby sitting uncomfortably on a bare examining-room table. The next slide showed Patty a few months later. She'd had radiation therapy. She was bald from the cyclophosphamide and fat in the face like a Buddha from the steroids. "She did well. We treated her for two years. Here she is today, three years after stopping therapy." The last slide showed a lovely seven-year-old child with long blond braids, proudly holding the leash of a cocker spaniel puppy.

"How did you decide upon two years of therapy?" a doctor in the audience asked.

"It's an arbitrary figure," the speaker answered. "Two or three years is the length of time we decided to treat the children. You can see from this slide of long-term survivors that it doesn't make any difference statistically. There must be a cutoff point. The therapy is far from harmless.

"Here is Jerry, age nine at time of diagnosis of lymphocytic leukemia." The slide of Jerry showed a thin, redheaded child with large bruises under his eyes. The next picture of Jerry had been taken one year later when he was in his first relapse. He looked sad and scared. Another slide showed Jerry after three more years, now off all treatment, with no signs of the disease. Then the surprise—Jerry, nineteen years old, a thin young man sitting on a motorcycle. Standing, next to him, one arm possessively around his shoulder, was a pretty girl. In her other arm she held a chubby redheaded baby.

"Several of the children from our first series have already become parents. There is no higher incidence of birth defects in their children than in the general population."

There were more pictures and more proof that childhood cancer was no longer a death sentence. The last case in the series of pictures was Saul. The first slide showed him at fifteen, a dark-eyed adolescent with pimples on his face, about to have his leg amputated for bone cancer. Next, Saul six months later, sitting on an examining-room table, the bare stump of his amputated leg sticking straight out. He was treated with chemotherapy for three years. There had been no recurrence of the cancer.

"I saved this picture of Saul, taken just a few months ago, for last, to make your lunch more enjoyable." The speaker turned back to the screen to look at it also. The full-length picture showed a handsome young man, black bearded and smiling, standing jauntily on a city street. His pants hid his artificial leg. The clothes he was wearing undoubtedly looked familiar to some of the doctors in the audience; white shirt and a white jacket with a distinctive red caduceus on the sleeve. It was the jacket of an intern at a New York City hospital.

"Saul today is an intern at Bellevue. I really enjoyed writing his recommendation for medical school. He is going to specialize in obstetrics."

The lights were switched on. We stood up to go to the dining room. The projector hadn't been turned off. Saul's picture still dominated the auditorium. This young man who was cured of cancer would spend his life bringing new life safely into the world. Years ago he would have been just one more fatal statistic.

My eyes met those of a young doctor who had been seated near me. "Right on," he said, smiling back at the screen.

During lunch one of the speakers was seated at my table. Over coffee he complimented us on our attention during his talk.

"That was a remarkable group of slides," I said. "Seeing the pictures of children who surely would have been dead if they had developed cancer ten years earlier is like watching some marvelous fantasy, a sort of *Bridge of San Luis Rey* in reverse."

"Not all the children live. But our cure rates get better and better."

"I have a patient," I told him, "who came down with acute lymphocytic leukemia when he was two and a half years old. We treated him longer than you recommend, but we were reluctant to stop therapy when he was doing so well. But we finally did. He was all right for five months,

138

and then he relapsed in his testes and his bone marrow. Now he's not responding to any therapy. What can be expected?"

The researcher stirred his coffee slowly. "If it were bone marrow alone, it might not be too bad. But testicular and bone-marrow relapse together—six months, a year at the longest."

"What if we had irradiated his testes at the start of the disease the way we did his brain. Would that have prevented the relapse?"

"We don't do that," the speaker answered. "When the boy grows up, how could you justify having sterilized him? What would you say to him? There's no way you could prove that had been necessary to save his life."

"But my patient may never grow up now," I persisted. "Would he have if we had irradiated his testes?"

Shocked at my words, the man looked carefully at me before he responded. "We can't predict which child is going to relapse. Would you sterilize all boys who would never relapse to save one who might?"

There was my answer. It did not surprise me, nor in my despair about David's relapse did it quell my anger. Anger at his testes for harboring the malignant cells for weeks or months or who knows how long before there were enough of them for us to notice. Anger at my profession for not recommending the testes be irradiated, and anger at myself for having used the word "cured" to his parents. For believing it myself. For now having to prepare for his death.

Many other doctors left the conference elated. These recent advances in cancer therapy were thrilling. But I returned to David with little hope for his life.

o   o   o

David now came to my office once a week. He'd gone to school a few times, but it tired him badly. He looked so ill his classmates were frightened. We arranged for a home teacher to come to his house every day. She asked me how much work she should give him. Did I ever expect him to rejoin his class?

"No," I said sadly, "but he must continue with his schoolwork. Taking it away from him would be like telling him he was going to die."

Now when he came into the office he needed my help to climb onto the examining-room table. He was embarrassed by his weakness. In his thin face, his smile had lost none of its sweetness.

He knew his disease was back, and he knew it was leukemia. I wondered if he had ever seen a television program about anyone dying from leukemia. I wondered if he thought this was happening to him. I hadn't said anything to him about dying. For that matter, I hadn't said anything to his parents, either.

I examined him and treated him and waited for a sign of response to therapy. There was none. Dr. Malick came up with a course of new drugs. We had to put David in the hospital for this. He would be there one week. Docilely, without any questions, he went into the hospital.

I saw him twice a day. Watching television or working on his schoolwork, he sat quietly in bed, never even complaining about the intravenous line in his arm. He always smiled when I entered the room, and I could have cried.

The new drugs didn't work. He now began to lose ground rapidly. His face developed a hectic flush. He ran a constant fever.

I started treatment with massive doses of antibiotics. The fever went away, but David was left with little energy. He slept more and more.

How, I wondered, would he die? I hoped he would slip into a coma and never know what was happening. I'd seen children die from bleeding, terrified as they vomited gushes of blood. I'd seen them die from pneumonia, gasping for breath. I'd seen children die in hospital beds, away from their parents, heavily sedated to ease their fear and loneliness. There was no longer any possibility in my mind that David might live. I was miserable at the thought of having to tell him he was going to die soon.

Would it be better just to let the disease take its course and not upset David by telling him what was going to happen? Wouldn't it be easier? Easier for me certainly, I thought, but didn't David deserve more from me? Surely deceit at the end was wrong. Or was it? After all, he was only a child. I wrestled with these thoughts every day, and every time I saw him he was weaker and weaker. What I wanted was a miracle, for him to rally, for one of the drugs to work, for me not to have to tell him he was dying.

I thought of David's trust, the hallmark of his character. He had trusted me to take care of him. I felt my failure with a despair that nothing could erase.

I hated the thought of his death so much it made me feel ill, and yet I had to recognize that there was absolutely nothing more I could do for him medically.

Although no patient of mine had died since my housestaff days, I had been on hospital duty and present when other doctors' patients had died. But those patients had not been children whom I had known for years. I had never loved any of them the way I loved David. There had never been any question as to whether the hospital was the best place for them to die. It was the expected place.

On occasion when a child was dying from a sudden catastrophic illness or an accident, I had put him on a respirator with the hope that keeping his blood oxygenated for a little while longer might give his body a chance to rally. But sometimes I'd made this decision just to give the dying child's parents a little more time to adjust to the tragedy. I had also given cardiac massage to revive dying children, hoping for that rare miracle of recovery in the very face of death.

The parents were always sent out of the room when this was done. When a child with an illness of long duration whom I was not going to resuscitate started to die, I also asked his parents to leave the room. It seemed kinder not to have them witness the actual moment of their child's death.

With David's death a certainty, I relived the misery I had felt when other children died and I worried about what to do for him now. I knew how much David dreaded being in the hospital. I, too, hated being a hospital patient and had absolutely no intention of dying in one. As an adult I expected to be given a choice when that time came. Didn't David deserve the same consideration? Wouldn't a death without needles, without oxygen masks, without any medical struggle to prolong his life be most decent? Wouldn't dying in the security of his own home be kinder?

David's parents saw that he was dying as clearly as I did. The new course of anti-leukemic drugs was completed. It would be several weeks before we could tell if they had any effect, but I had no genuine hope. We were all bitterly crushed. The unthinkable had become the inevitable over just a few months. Betty and Stan did not ask me if he was going to die. They waited for me to tell them. If he were to die in his own home, the task of caring for him would fall mainly on Betty. I had to give Betty and Stan a clear idea of what might happen so they could make the decision as to where their son was to die.

I gave David another transfusion and sent him home.

○　○　○

Late one afternoon I asked Betty and Stan to come to my office. Finally I had to tell them there was no hope, there was nothing further I could do for David. Until that was said, there was no way we could plan for his death. I was terribly depressed. By admitting that there was nothing more I could do for David, I felt I was no longer needed. Yet on a deeper level I realized I was needed more than ever.

We sat in front of the window in my office for a few minutes and watched the shadows lengthen on the hills. I finally broke the silence. "David gets closer to death each day. I've said nothing to him about dying. I must soon. I've always been uncomfortable watching the children who die in the hospital. It seems to me that children hate being in the hospital and would be much more at peace in their own homes. Before I tell David he's dying I want to know what your feelings are about where he should die."

Betty reached out for her husband's hand. Tears filled her eyes. "We want David where it is best for him, if we can manage it. What's liable to happen?"

"I don't really know. Often a child goes into a coma and just dies without knowing it. This can occur suddenly if there is a brain hemorrhage. If that happens I think it would be best to have him in the hospital. Sometimes they vomit a lot of blood or convulse or can't breathe. I can be at your house within half an hour anytime, maybe even sooner. Or you could call an ambulance. But we need to plan so you know which way to turn, even though we don't know what is going to happen." I felt less and less sure that what I was saying was right.

I was looking at Betty as I talked. She looked as if she might faint. She held tightly to Stan's hand. I hesitated and then said, "Let's do this. We'll keep him at home, and then if it doesn't work out, I'll put him in the hospital."

Betty nodded, tears prevented her from speaking.

"We want him with us at home," said Stan.

o   o   o

It wasn't just David I thought about so often these days. John and Mary occupied my thoughts, too. David was John's idol and his chief competitor. What effect was David's death going to have on John? If David died at home where John could see him, at least there would be no mystery. If David died with the same grace with which he had lived, wouldn't it give John confidence? Wouldn't it give us all something we were lacking?

I was right to be worried about John. Just recently his behavior had become a real problem. He'd turned sullen. Many times over the past years he'd come along to my office and sat quietly while I gave my attention to his brother. Betty didn't believe in spoiled children. Her three had been raised to have good manners and consideration for each other. Despite his illness David had never been catered to. John, never as calm as David, required a firmer hand, which he got. However, I could always see that he was a bit jealous of David. There had been a long period when we had considered David cured. Betty had had lots of time for John then. When David relapsed she suddenly had to spend all day at the hospital. John scarcely saw her for several weeks. More important, the depression and sorrow that overwhelmed both his parents shut John even further away from them.

John did what you might expect. He became mischievous and got into fights. He teased and hit his sister. Little Mary had an easygoing, loving temperament. She was wrapped up with her dolls and her little friends. She was sad that David was sick, but it didn't disturb her world. But David's illness disturbed John's world, and he, in turn, set out to disturb everyone around him.

Children are the true weathervanes of a family. When things are steady, they turn without effort in the right direction. When problems make life stormy, they spin out of control. It's routine to say to a mother whose child is showing disturbing behavior, "Can you spend more time with him? Can you make sure that time is of the best and most loving quality?"

But what was I to say to Betty? Her firstborn was getting weaker day by day. More and more of her time was required to care for him and to bring him to my office for treatment or blood transfusions. Her fear of David's approaching death, her anxiety about what was to happen next depleted what energy she had.

I couldn't say to her, "Spend more time with John." Every minute of her day, and then some, was already accounted for.

Perhaps there was a way for me to talk to John that might make a difference. His brother's illness had in a very real sense robbed him of his mother's attention.

"Betty," I said as we sat in my office waiting for David's transfusion to finish, "can you get a neighbor to stay with David tomorrow and take John out of school and bring him to my office?"

"Sure," she said. "But why?"

"I'd like to talk with John and let him know what's happening. Perhaps if he understands he'll calm down and change his behavior. It's worth a try. I'd like to reassure you that I don't consider his lying and fighting as something you have to be seriously concerned about. It's resentment that David's getting so much attention and so much of you. And I don't see how you could find any more time for John right now. But you might tell him how sad you are and what a big help he is to you. I think we should tell John that David's going to die very soon. But I've not talked to David yet about dying—have you?"

As soon as I said this, I was ashamed of myself. How could I have expected her to talk to David about dying? I had avoided any mention of it with him because it was just too painful for me. Instead I'd told him he needed new kinds of medicine, which must have made him think that he would get well again. I'd encouraged him to keep up with his schoolwork. By implication I had encouraged him to live. What would happen when David realized I was not telling the truth about his getting well? Unless all of us were willing to talk about death in a natural manner, we wouldn't be able to accept the reality of it, and neither would David.

I was terribly worried about David's dying at home. To tell the truth, I was afraid he would not lapse into a coma, which was the kind of death I could handle most easily. I was afraid he would suffer. I was afraid I would not be able to find a medicine to relieve his pain. Most of all, perhaps, I was afraid that having him die in his home would be a horrendous experience for everyone, regardless of what was best for David. I could avoid this by putting him in the hospital. He would soon be too weak to object. He would sink into that predeath depression I had seen so many times, unwilling to talk, disinterested in his surroundings, withdrawn and depressed for his remaining days. That part of dying I was familiar with. That was what always happened in the hospital.

I didn't want that to happen to David. I didn't want him to die the way Sara, a ten-year-old girl with leukemia, had recently died in our hospital.

Sara had had leukemia for less than two years. Her course was never as hopeful as David's. She relapsed early after her initial remission. Her parents couldn't accept this and took her away from medical care to a faith healer. After a few months, when Sara was desperately ill, they came back to their doctor, who put Sara in the hospital. She was close to death. Her parents still prayed for miracles. When it became obvious that one was not going to materialize, her mother was so distraught she could scarcely bear to be around Sara and spent most of her visiting time standing outside Sara's room crying. Sara spent most of her time inside her room crying. It was a terrible situation, and our

146

hospital nurses were very upset by it. The night Sara died a nurse was with her. Sara's mother was at home under heavy sedation.

Sara told the nurse, "Please let me go home. I'll be good. I won't be any trouble. I want my mother." The nurse was so shaken after Sara died that she had to be sent home.

That must not be allowed to happen to David. I thought of how bravely he used to hold out his little arm for the injections when he was only three years old. We must help him now. And that had to be set up before he became so sick he couldn't tell us where he wanted to be. Knowing David, I felt that if I put him in the hospital, he would accept it without protest even if his heart was breaking.

Originally I'd interpreted John's bad behavior as a reaction to his lack of time with his mother. Now I wasn't sure. Could it be that this inarticulate child was angry because he was being excluded from this serious family matter? Could his anger be dissipated by being honest with him?

The next day Betty brought John to see me. He and I had never had a private conversation. He came into the office timidly. He had none of the steady confidence that was David's most charming trait. I remembered how he had fought every time he'd needed an injection when he was smaller. Even recently John had asked hostilely when he saw me, "Do I have to have a shot?" although he knew only David got the injections.

This morning he sat down on a little stool and scooted around the room. I reached out and took both his hands in mine, as much to hold him still as to get his attention.

"John, what's going on?"

"Nothing." He giggled and looked at the floor.

"John, we have a problem and I want you to know about it. Your mother has to spend all of her time with David these days. Have you any idea why? Do you know what's wrong?"

Instantly I had John's attention. "David's sick," he said. And then with a directness that took my breath away he added, "Is he going to die?"

"Yes, John, he's going to die."

John sat absolutely still. He looked frightened. Big tears gathered in his eyes. "Did I do it to him?" he asked in a quavering voice, and he started to cry. "Is it my fault?"

"No, John," I said, gathering him into my arms. "It's not your fault, even if you sometimes wished him dead when you were angry. It's no one's fault. All of us will die someday when it's our time. I will, you will, your mommy will—this is just David's time."

John clung to me. It was all I could do not to cry with him, but I held him and stroked his hair and waited for him to stop crying.

Finally he did and released his grip on me. He drew back. "Will it hurt?"

"I don't know," I said, thinking I'd better be completely honest. "I hope not, but I don't know. There are medicines I can give him, so it shouldn't hurt. I think it will be just like going to sleep. But he'll need a lot of care until he dies. And your mother needs a lot of help now. She's very sad, and she's very tired, too. She has to take care of David, and soon he may not even be able to get out of bed. Do you think you can help her?"

John nodded. "Does David know he's going to die?" he asked. "His kitten got hit by a car and she died. There was lots of blood. Mommy put her in a box and we dug a hole in the backyard. David said she was going to heaven. Is that what happens when you die?"

My impulse to just say yes was stopped by the way John was looking at me. Why had I never noticed this quality of intellectual daring, this direct demand for answers that John was showing. Loving David with the intensity I did, I'd simply not paid much attention to his very different brother.

148

"Maybe it is. I don't really know. Some people are sure you go to heaven when you die." John took his intense gaze off me for a minute. "Other people think maybe we come back as flowers or animals, or even other people. But, John, I only know we must help David, for he won't be with us very much longer."

Was John only five years old? Minutes earlier he'd been scooting about the room like a three year old. I'd thought, I'm making a mistake. He's much too young to understand what I want to say to him, too self-centered with the natural selfishness of childish emotions, to do anything but go his irritating way while his brother dies.

I knew now I'd been wrong. Although I'd finished talking, John remained still. He'd put his hands in mine again, but while I'd taken his at first to get his attention, he now held mine as a bond between us. He looked sincerely into my eyes.

"I can help lots," he said simply.

o o o

One week passed. My notes in David's clinic chart were brief—his white count, the absence of fever, the size of his enlarging spleen. One line said, "David is to die at home. All care will be given in the clinic or the emergency room of the hospital."

His weight loss made him look old. His eyes, once a lively deep brown, became his most prominent feature, but gone was their liveliness. His expression, previously so trusting, was now uneasy. I hadn't told David yet that he was going to die. I was waiting for the proper moment. I hoped I would recognize it and react truthfully when it came.

David grew weaker. His home teacher still came to his house three mornings a week. She told me in confidence that it was just to see him. There was no point to trying to teach him anything any longer, with death so imminent. She came because she loved him.

He was terribly anemic and had to come to the clinic for blood transfusions frequently. His platelet count was so dangerously low he could bleed into his brain at any time. Betty told me he spent most of his time at home lying in bed. Usually with him, curled in his arms, slept the new kitten, a replacement for the one buried in the backyard. He'd given it the same name.

Although his face was pathetically thin and drawn, he smiled his slow, sweet smile whenever he saw me.

o   o   o

Dr. Malick telephoned me one afternoon. "I've just come from a conference at the medical school," he said. "There is a new combination of drugs they've had some good results with. I want to admit David to the hospital and try them."

"What's the point of any more treatment?" I asked with barely disguised anger. "What about their side effects? Will they make him bleed or give him cramps? I think having to put him back in the hospital to treat him one last time is a bad idea. You don't really expect anything to work at this point, do you?"

There was shocked silence from Dr. Malick. "They probably won't work. But suppose they do? We must try everything. At best they might arrest the disease for a while longer. You know, you're too involved with this patient and it's affecting your judgment. I'd like you to admit him to the hospital tomorrow morning."

"How long will this treatment take?" I asked.

"Four days."

"I'm going to send him home at the end of that time even if he has to be carried out."

"That," said Malick, "will have to be your decision."

o o o

Once again David was admitted to the hospital. He was sitting up in bed looking out the window when I came to see him. "You told me I wouldn't be in the hospital anymore," he said miserably.

It was the first time I'd ever heard him complain. He looked scared.

"David, this is for only four days. Not one minute longer. As soon as the last dose of medicine is given, you'll go home. That isn't so long, is it?"

But those four days could be an eternity. He knew he wasn't getting better. I must tell him he was dying. He didn't question why we were treating him again. Medicine, transfusions, intravenous injections had become a way of life for him. I'd never asked him if he wanted an injection. Of course he didn't, but he never objected. I couldn't let him guess that I considered this latest series of drugs a waste of his precious remaining time.

What folly, I thought bitterly, a doctor's inability to give up, ever, ever.

"Only four days, David," I said, and kissed him as I left.

David had never been withdrawn on any of his previous hospital stays. This time was different. He didn't complain; he simply withdrew quietly. The first day he refused to eat his dinner. His mother went out and bought him a hamburger. It lay untasted on the side of his bed, and in a little while he threw it in the wastebasket. He turned on his side with his face toward the wall and closed his eyes. He's just worn out and upset about being in the hospital, I thought. He'll be more his old self tomorrow. But tomorrow he was no better. The next day I sat on the side of his bed and stroked his hair. It had lost all its luster.

"David, one whole day is over. There are only three more to go and then you'll be home again."

He nodded.

"Does your tummy hurt?"

He nodded again.

"Well, I have something to stop the tummy ache. It tastes pretty bad, but you can wash it down with juice. I don't want you to have a tummy ache," I said, thinking of the mass I had felt enlarging around his appendix. A few days earlier when I palpated his lower abdomen, it had been tender. I could make out a very small lump in the area of his appendix. Had he been a healthy child, I would have diagnosed a ruptured appendix and called a surgeon immediately. Since it was David, I was sure the appendix was ruptured, but there was nothing any surgeon could do. To operate on a child who may bleed profusely was out of the question. I started treating the appendix with large doses of antibiotics, hoping this might control it for a while. The antibiotics had to be given intravenously every two hours. I worried about how we would manage this when he went home.

Time was clearly running out.

I took his frail body in my arms and cradled his head against me. "David, most of the time when we're sick, we take medicine and it makes us better. But sometimes the medicine doesn't work and we don't get well. We die." I felt his body tense. I held him closely and rocked him as if he were a baby. "I'm going to die someday, and your mommy is going to die someday, too. Usually mommies die before their children, but sometimes—sometimes—" My voice

failed me. I kissed the top of his head and saw my tears fall
on his hair. His arms were around me. He tightened them as
he nestled closer.

"Am I going to die?" he asked, his voice muffled against
me.

"Yes, David."

"Does my mommy know?"

"Yes, and John and your daddy know, even Mary. They
want you at home with them."

"Will it hurt?" asked this child who had never let us
know he was frightened.

"No, I don't think so. It'll just be like going to sleep.
And your mommy will be with you."

We held each other in a profound silence. I realized
with wonder that what I had said had not shocked him at
all. Why had I waited so long, making excuses to myself that
I needed the perfect moment? There is no such thing as the
perfect moment. We make all our moments, and by the
truth and love we bring to them, we make them perfect.
David had probably thought he was dying for at least a
month, maybe longer. His innate sensitivity had made him
keep that from us.

My arms were cramped. "Is there anything you want?"
I asked, shifting his weight.

"Would you rub my back?" he said. "It hurts."

I couldn't save him, and I couldn't tell him what death
was like. But I could rub his back.

o   o   o

David failed rapidly. I was afraid he wasn't going to
live through the next two days of therapy. That night when
I left the hospital David was asleep, drugged with the solution of morphine and cocaine I had ordered.

The following morning when I came in, his face was turned to the wall. No, said the nurse, he hadn't asked for any of the pain medicine. No, he hadn't wanted breakfast. I leaned over him. He opened his eyes briefly and turned his face from me. Betty was sitting in a chair by his bed, pale and worn out. She'd been there all night.

"He won't talk to me. He won't even look at me," she said despairingly. "He seems to have lost all will to live."

Despite the fact that I saw Betty every day, I had not mentioned the conversation I'd had with David about his death. It was simply too painful to me. I was appalled at the mistake I was sure I had made in telling him he was dying. What a fool I had been. Now he'd given up. How much better to have let him go gently. How cruel of me to have expected a child his age to want to live after I told him he was going to die. How unforgivably stupid of me.

"Betty," I said, "we promised him he would go home. He has a ruptured appendix and needs intravenous antibiotics. When you take him home tomorrow, you'll have to give them. Our nurse will teach you how to draw up the proper dose and put it in the intravenous line. I'm going to have the resident place a bit of intravenous tubing called a heparin lock permanently into a vein in his hand. That way when you give the antibiotics, you can stick the needle into the tubing, not into David. It won't hurt him and it'll be easy for you."

Betty nodded with relief. Here was something she could do.

"Here's the medicine for pain." I picked up a bottle that looked like any cough syrup. "It's morphine and cocaine. It will dull the pain. Don't wait for him to be hurting before you give it to him. Let him adjust the dose. Tomorrow the chemotherapy will be finished. You can take him home just as soon as the last dose is given. You'll probably have to carry him." She and I looked at each other and understood perfectly what we were doing.

I walked down the long hall toward the elevator. David's nurse caught up with me. "Are you really going to send him home?" she asked. "He's in terrible shape. He can't sit up or get out of bed. He won't eat or drink anything."

"He's going home tomorrow," I said shortly. "I promised him he'd go home." The nurse gave me a skeptical look and shrugged.

o   o   o

That night as I tossed restlessly in my bed I thought, he'll never live until tomorrow. What few good days he might have had left I've robbed him of, not only by this last therapy, but by telling him he was going to die. I lay awake most of the night waiting for the telephone to ring and the nurse's voice to tell me that David had died.

But the telephone didn't ring.

The next morning when I entered David's room, the intravenous line had been disconnected. The heparin lock was neatly taped in place in his hand.

"Are you actually discharging him?" asked the resident doctor.

"Yes."

"And his mother is going to treat his bloodstream infection? Isn't that asking a bit much of her?"

I didn't answer him.

"Why don't you keep him here a few weeks and treat him properly for the infection?" he persisted.

"Because he doesn't have a few weeks," I snapped. "He'll be treated just as properly at home as in the hospital. Does it matter whether a nurse or his mother injects the antibiotics? But even if we could clear up the bloodstream infection, it wouldn't save his life. If he doesn't go home today, I'm afraid he'll never go home again."

"He's your patient," the resident said sarcastically and walked away.

I wrote the discharge order. David, wrapped in a blanket, was carried out of the hospital in his father's arms. I didn't expect David to live through the night and I told this to Betty. "Call me when you need me," I said and I left.

I stayed home that night to be near the telephone. But Betty didn't call. The next morning I telephoned her from the office. With trepidation I asked, "How is he?"

"You won't believe this," Betty said, "but a change came over him as soon as he got home. While David was in the hospital Stan moved out all the dining-room furniture and put David's bed and toys in there. I'm usually in the kitchen, and David's bedroom had been at the very back of the house. The dining room is at the front and its windows are low so you can see the street easily. David was really pleased. He went to sleep and when he woke up he not only got out of bed but he actually walked to the window. He asked for something to eat and later he even went outside and sat on the lawn for a little while. I can't believe it."

"Oh, Betty," I said, "we did the right thing—we really did! I'll be out there at noon."

o   o   o

The Carvers' house was at the foothills to the mountains that I loved to watch so much from my office window. The road wound for fifteen miles through farmlands and orchards, past fields of green alfalfa. The noon sun brightened the golden hills. A wild rabbit darted safely across the road in front of my car into a field where two brown horses stood sleepily together, one's neck across the other's back. If one could live on earth for only eight years, then this was the place to have done it, I thought. I hoped Stan had driven home slowly so David could see it all once more.

I knocked on the door of a small brick house. As I waited, I could see through the low front window David sitting on the edge of his bed, trying to tie a doll's hat on the head of a sleepy kitten. Betty answered the door. She hugged me, smiling. John gave me a hug, too, and dashed outside. Mary came in soaking wet from running through a neighbor's sprinkler with her friends. I walked into David's new room. The child sitting on the edge of the bed playing with the kitten bore little resemblance to the withdrawn, depressed boy who had turned his face to the wall in the hospital just twenty-four hours earlier.

"He's eaten two little snacks," said Betty. "And he drinks juice, and even goes to the bathroom without help. He stays in bed most of the time, but he seems so much better."

For a minute my heart leaped as I thought, is it possible the last course of therapy is really working? Is David getting better? Had Malick been right? But this thought died even as it was born. What was different wasn't his pathetically wasted body but his spirit. He was comfortable and no longer fearful. How can one describe "vibes"? You can't hear them or touch them, but you can certainly feel them. They're as real as barometric pressure. This was still the same child, but he was where he longed to be, and the vibes were good. For David the vibes in the hospital had been terrible.

Now that I was here, what was I to do? First, see how Betty mixed up the antibiotics and gave the injection. Our nurse had trained her well. Alcohol sponge on the top of the vial, inject in a bit of air, withdraw the medicine, check the syringe. Then with the proficiency of a trained nurse, swab off the heparin lock and inject the antibiotic into her son. David watched his mother proudly.

"Didn't know what a good nurse your mother is, did you?" I said, and we were rewarded with his wonderful smile.

I saw no reason to examine him. I'd come to his home to give my love and support, not medical care.

So instead of David I examined the kitten. I checked her eyes and ears and chest and tummy, and David held her and laughed. The kitten, floppy little thing, tolerated this without scratching. I told David he had a very good baby, and he asked if I would give her shots next time. What a father he would have made!

All that week I came to see him every afternoon at lunchtime. One day I did examine him. The abscess around his appendix felt as large as a grapefruit. Nevertheless, he was able to get up and walk. He could still go to the bathroom unaided. How he did this with such an abscess I couldn't imagine.

"How much morphine is he taking?" I asked.

"He asks for a spoonful maybe every three or four hours. He's never asked for more than one teaspoonful. He says that stops the pain right away."

That was very little morphine. Such an abscess should make it impossible for him to move, and yet it didn't seem to bother him. I was truly amazed.

o   o   o

On the weekend I drove from my home to his. One of my younger children wanted to come with me. She would be very quiet, she said.

"Is he really going to die?" she asked me. "What does he look like? Does his mother cry all the time? Could we bring him a present?"

A present? On a Sunday, to a child who was going to live only a few days? What did she want to give him? She went and fetched a book of poems, ragged from much handling and reading. Her favorite book.

"Sure," I said. "We'll read him some poems."

David was in bed when we got there. He was weaker. He'd developed an itchy rash. I knew it had to be an allergic reaction to the antibiotics. Why did I have him on them, anyway? What was the purpose of trying to control the infection at this point? The rash meant I had to stop them, but I'd leave the heparin lock in place in case I decided to give him another transfusion. And why would I want to do that, I thought? To make him feel better, I decided. I'll treat him as long as it makes him feel better.

My daughter's book was a wonderful idea. As the antibiotics had given Betty something to do for him, the book now gave me something to do for him. I opened it to a poem about Christopher Robin when he was sick. David smiled as I read,

Christopher Robin
Had wheezles
And sneezles,
They bundled him
Into
His bed.
They gave him what goes
With a cold in the nose,
And some more for a cold
In the head.

"It's Chip's favorite book, David. She wants you to have it. I'll read it to you every afternoon."

How many afternoons did he have left? Day after day I

drove to his house. We developed a routine. John would answer the doorbell, give me a hug and tag along after me into David's room to hear the poems also. I would give David a kiss and sit on the edge of his bed. David would pick the poem. "Read me about John-John Morrison-Morrison," he'd say, looking at his brother. John would sit on the floor by my feet, his hand about my ankle. Anything for contact.

Occasionally I felt David's abdomen. The abscess was larger. How he managed to walk was beyond me. The morphine worked well.

After my visit Betty and I usually went outside together, sometimes just to my car, but more often we walked around the block. We didn't say much, just walked for relief. We walked past flower gardens blooming as they would continue to bloom once David was dead. Children played on the lawns. Cats basked in the sunshine. It was lovely, it was all so alive. This should have been David's.

A few more days passed. When David stood up now, the abscess made a bulge that showed through his pajamas. He slept more and more and ran a constant fever. I gave him another blood transfusion.

One afternoon when I came to the house, David wasn't in his room. Betty led me into her bedroom. David lay curled up in the center of his parents' bed. He'd crept into their bed in the middle of the night. "We let him sleep with us and he hasn't been up this morning," she said.

I leaned over him. His breathing was rapid. His face was warm with fever. I sat beside him and listened to his chest with my stethoscope. My touch awakened him. He looked at me with recognition and smiled weakly. I stroked his hair. "Do you want a poem?" I asked softly. He nodded and closed his eyes.

I sat with my arm around him and read him a very

short one. He didn't seem to be listening. "Do you want another poem?" I asked. He shook his head and closed his eyes. I put my cheek against his and then kissed him. I tucked the covers loosely about him and walked out. I turned and looked back. I didn't expect ever to see him alive again.

Betty and I went out of the house. We stood in the middle of the lawn. Tears ran down our faces. We put our arms about each other. I could barely speak. "Betty, I think this is the time. I think he's dying now. I can't imagine he will live the night. I don't know what has kept him going this long. He is the sweetest, bravest child I've ever known—"

Near us the sunlight sparked on a patch of marigolds. Betty moved back from me. "I'm going to let him stay in bed with us," she said.

That night she slept with her arms about David, curled around him like a mother lion around her cub. He slept quietly and scarcely moved at all. The next afternoon when I came to the house, he was lying in the middle of the big bed curled up like a fetus. I sat down next to him. Although he was aware of me, he didn't speak. I looked at him for a long, long time. Something about him was different. Some transformation had taken place during the night.

Yesterday his face had looked drawn. It now seemed beautiful in its delicacy. His skin was almost transparent. His eyes were luminous, and there was an ethereal quality about him. And yet I sensed a distance between us that was entirely new. I laid my hand gently on his arm. He smiled very slightly, then turned his head from me as if I no longer mattered. He wasn't dulled like a child in a coma or heavily drugged. It was as if he was turning his whole attention inward. I felt a sense of awe.

I took his hand in mine. He held my fingers loosely,

with just barely enough pressure to let me know he recognized me. But after a few minutes he removed his fingers from mine and closed his eyes. It was as if he'd said, "You may leave me now."

I kissed him and left the room. I asked Betty how much of the morphine he was taking.

"Very little," she said, "even less than when he first came home."

The next three days David still managed to get up to go to the bathroom. Occasionally he would ask for some juice or morphine. But in a sense he left us three days before he died. You could tell it required great effort for him to ask for anything or answer us, and he made this effort as seldom as possible.

Betty and David slept those last nights together as close at the time of his dying as they had been before his birth when she carried him inside her. During the day, she told me, she would often go in and sit by him and watch him. Just sit for hours without a thought that she could recall. She loved him then with an intensity that she'd never experienced before in her life, and she got from him as he lay dying the feeling that she'd been singled out for one of the most precious gifts in the world—having had David for eight years.

⁂ ⁂ ⁂

On Saturday morning when Stan was home from work, David awakened, once again inexplicably interested in his surroundings. He got out of the big bed and went to the bathroom and then walked back to his own bed in the dining room. He lay down but didn't fall asleep. Betty was surprised by this and heartened by the fact that he was up again. She'd scarcely left his side for three days. She thought, he's so alert he can't possibly die right now. She kissed him on his forehead and asked, "Is it all right if I go shopping for a little while?" He touched her hand and nodded his head. She noticed that his dark eyes seemed more beautiful than ever. She left, anxious to get the shopping over with and be back with him.

David lay on his bed and looked out of the window. He could see his sister playing on the front lawn. The kitten was on the window sill, trying to catch a fly.

After a little while David asked his father for some morphine. He swallowed a spoonful and made a face. He asked for some juice. Stan went to the kitchen to get some from the refrigerator. He could see David all the time. David was lying on his back on the bed. He held his hands up in front of his face, looking at them. He stretched out his arms and then brought his hands in close to his eyes. He seemed to be examining each finger the way a baby does when it first discovers its hands.

Stan turned his attention to pouring the juice. When he brought it to the bed, David was dead.

David hadn't made a sound. His father couldn't believe it. He sat by David, almost expecting him to breathe again. David's eyes were closed. He looked as if he had just fallen asleep.

Stan sat by David for a while and then went outside and called Mary and John. The two children went to the bed where the body of their dead brother lay. Mary ran her finger along David's arm and put her head down next to his on the pillow. John stood looking at David and then went to the window and picked up the kitten. He brought the kitten to the bed and curled it up next to David, placing his dead brother's arm around the kitten in the position it had rested so often.

When Betty came home that was how she found her family.